DATE DUE

MAR - 5 1997	

French Women Writers and the Book

Penelope Writing. Early sixteenth-century illustration. Reprinted by courtesy of the Bibliothèque Nationale, Paris.

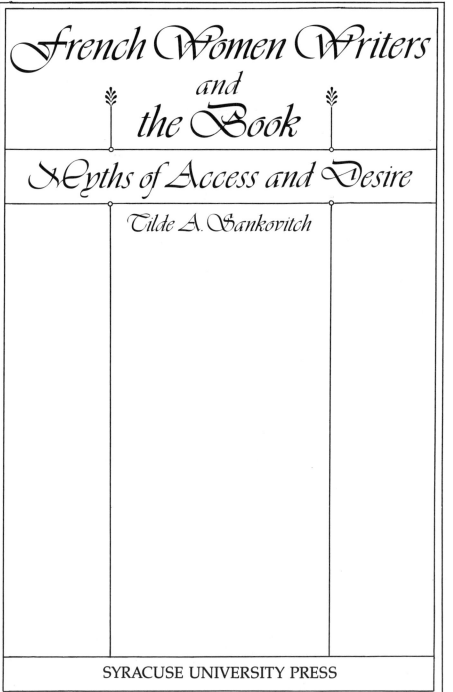

French Women Writers
and
the Book

Myths of Access and Desire

Tilde A. Sankovitch

SYRACUSE UNIVERSITY PRESS

Copyright © 1988 by Syracuse University Press
Syracuse, New York 13244-5160

All Rights Reserved

First published 1988
First Edition

93 92 91 90 89 88   6 5 4 3 2 1

The paper used in this publication meets the minimum requirements of American National Standard for Information Sciences—Permanence of Paper for Printed Library Materials, ANSI Z39.48-1984. ∞ ™

Library of Congress Cataloging-in-Publication Data

Sankovitch, Tilde.
  French women writers and the book: myths of access
  and desire
  Tilde A. Sankovitch — 1st ed.
      p.   cm.
  Bibliography: p.
  Includes index.
  ISBN 0-8156-2431-X
      1. French literature—Women authors—History and
  criticism. 2. Women and literature—France—History.
  3. Myth in literature. 4. Women in literature. I. Title.
  PQ149.S26   1988
  840 '.9 '9287—dc19   87-33503
                                                          CIP

MANUFACTURED IN THE UNITED STATES OF AMERICA

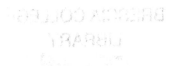

To the memory of
Norman B. Spector,
teacher
and
friend

Tilde A. Sankovitch is Professor in the Department of French and Italian at Northwestern University. She is the coeditor of *The Poems of the Troubador Bertran de Born* and has been a contributor to many books including *Women in the Middle Ages and Renaissance* (Syracuse University Press). She has also published numerous articles and reviews on medieval and Renaissance subjects.

Contents

$\mathcal{A}$cknowledgments

Part of this study was conducted during a leave granted me by North-western University. I want to thank the many friends and colleagues who have consistently supported me in my work, in particular Professors Arlene Daniels, Robert Lerner, William D. Paden, and Irwin Weil. Special thanks go to Prof. William Roberts, who generously gave his time and effort to help me find illustrations. I am deeply grateful to the Women of the Portia group in Evanston, Illinois, for their continuing interest and their pertinent suggestions. Finally, I wish to thank my three daughters, Anne-Marie, Natasha, and Nina, all lovers of and aspirants to the Book, and my husband, Tola; all were untiringly generous in giving me encouragement and love.

Introduction

And so I came home a woman starving for images
to say my hunger is so old so fundamental . . .

Adrienne Rich

. . . a book of myths in which our names do not
appear.

Adrienne Rich

Dis-eased and infected by the sentences of patriarchy, yet unable to deny the urgency of that
"poet-fire" she felt within herself, what strategies
did the woman writer develop for overcoming her
anxiety of authorship?

Sandra M. Gilbert, Susan Gubar

Myths are the answers to questions we, human creatures, ask. They are the meaningful stories we tell in order to explain, interpret, and arrange or rearrange our experiences, histories, contexts—ourselves. As such, myths and myth making correspond to our profound need for an ordered, acceptable view of the macrocosm of our universe, as well as of the microcosm of our own hearts and minds. Myths grow out of desire: we desire, we demand, to know about our human condition. Myths make us possible, our selves and our lives, as they offer us outlines, images, structures that reflect and reveal our past and our future possibilities. Myths contain us and liberate us, reassure us about our past and empower us to undertake the deeds of the future.

1

From this mythic world and its creation, woman has been largely excluded. Our western mythologies tend to be patriarchal ones, in which women figure as the malleable objects of an overwhelmingly male imagination, but seldom have the chance to be the composing/speaking/writing subjects of their own tales.

In his article, "Aristotle's Sister: A Poetics of Abandonment," Lawrence Lipking examines one emblematic moment of our cultural past: emblematic in that it illustrates to perfection the confinement to silence that has been woman's dominant pattern and lot, and the male right to the power of speech. It is an episode in Homer's *Odyssey* (I:325–59), in which Penelope asks the minstrel Phemius, who is entertaining the suitors in her palace, to change the subject of his tale—the Achaians' return from the Trojan war—because it is too painful to her. Her son, Telemachus, rebuffs her in a tirade which ends with these words: "Come into the house and apply yourself to work,/ To the loom and the distaff, and give orders to your servants/ To set at the work. This talk will concern all the men,/ But me especially. For the power in the house is mine."[1] The "talk" in question is the *mythos*, and, as Lipking comments, "*Mythos* is barred to women" (1983, 66). Both in the fatidic opposition and distance between "loom and distaff" on the one hand, and *mythos* (i.e., word, speech, tale, myth) on the other and in women's disbarment from the latter, this episode is emblematic indeed, encapsulating centuries of similar distinctions between female and male activity, and of interdictions against women who desire, who need, and who claim their autonomous access to myth.

Lipking points out that, in the *Odyssey*, Penelope does get her will; the singer stops singing, but only because the suitors, inflamed by the sight of her beauty, start clamoring to possess her, and their avid noises drown out the song of Phemius. If Penelope therefore seems to have gotten her way, it is not through a voiced and accepted articulation of her will, not through the imposition of her discourse, but through the impact of her sexuality. Penelope *is* sex, as in French the term for women as a group is "le sexe." Sex—that is, what makes woman subservient to a patriarchal scheme of male desire and female reproductivity—is what defines her, not reason, imagination, or feeling, nor her own desire.

The passage from the *Odyssey* also makes it clear where power resides, and it is not on the side of woman and her claims: impotent, she may only do as she is told, that is, limit herself to the restricted milieu and tasks assigned her by man. Telemachus's words leave no doubt about this; they illustrate the male appropriation of power inherent in *mythos*. It is the power to give shape and impact to one's being through words; to fashion and "read" one's experience through stories. It is the power not only to comprehend the past but to validate and justify the present, and to project oneself into the future. It is the power to create a precursor for those who will come after, to establish a pattern, to invent appropriate names and images corresponding to one's knowledge of oneself, and to leave these names and images as beacons for others.

The very possibility of gaining knowledge of oneself is bound up with the access to myth, as self-discovery and self-formulation are complementary and indeed inseparable activities. This was understood by the poet Rimbaud who, in his famous 1871 letter to his friend Paul Demeny, wrote about the creative joy and the poetic necessity of witnessing "the *eclosion* of my thought: I look at it, I listen to it." He goes on to claim that, before he gained this crucial self-possession, his self had only been known in its "false meanings," since its true, authentic significance had been repressed by the "old imbeciles" (Rimbaud [1871] 1981, 347)—that is, the stifling forces of tradition and conventionality; they had kept him from "the first [i.e., the most basic, most important] study of the person who wants to be a poet . . . the knowledge of himself, whole; he seeks his soul, he inspects it, he tries it out, he learns it" (Rimbaud [1871] 1981, 348). Rimbaud extends the vision of that self-learning, indispensable to self-expression, to women: "When woman's unmeasured bondage shall be broken, when she shall live for and through herself, man—hitherto detestable—having let her go, she, too, will be poet! Woman will find the unknown" ([1871] 1981, 348).[2]

Woman *is* the unknown, and such knowledge of herself and her condition as she may have is repressed in the stories told by and for men. The raw elements of cosmic, physical, and psychic reality were and are accessible to both sexes, but the form giving, the interpretation—and thus the clear, lucid apprehension of that material—only to one.

As a secondary component of the male universe, often beloved—even adored—certainly admired, yet also feared and hated, woman does appear in male myths, but in forms, figures, and images that are not hers, and do not reflect her adequately or accurately. When women show up in the books of male myths it is under names they themselves do not recognize, springing from an alien naming, and clad in deceptive images equally alien to what they gropingly know and intuitively feel to be true about themselves. Thus, even when they seem to be present in male myths, their presence is a mock presence. Women are really absent from them, since only false names, false icons, inane and without reverberation or deep radiance, pretend to represent women. Mary Daly denounces what she calls patriarchy's "deadly deception: mystification through myth" (1978, 43), and the "dismemberment" (1978, 73), the mutilation of her being, that male-invented myths inflict upon woman. Authors such as Simone de Beauvoir, and others after her, too numerous to name, have exposed some of these myths and the nefarious processes of mythification by which women have been defined, and which have, in many cases, become part and parcel of our cultural heritage. To give just a few examples, woman has been iconized as the fearful and fascinating temptress, the *femme fatale*; as the passive erotic object, the *odalisque*; as the pure, ministering, loving, all-forgiving angel; as the earth-mother, wide and deep source of life and death; as the Christian polarities of the Virgin and the Whore; and as a whole catalog of bodily parts, separated, *blason*-like, from any possible integration into a complete human being, monstrously enlarged in their obsessive and exclusive specificity: Lips, Lap, Womb (including the *Vagina Dentata* of male nightmares), Genitalia, Breasts.[3]

Many of these mythic constructs are surrounded by an appealing aura of scabrous or saintly, idealizing glory, or at least by an odor of flattering mystery, so that women themselves have been seduced into becoming the accomplices of the myths that deprive them of their identity and incarcerate them in inauthenticity: the shams offered them seem so provocative, so scintillating, so prestigious, so interesting above all! As Rita Dove writes in her poem, "Canary": "If you can't be free, be a mystery" (1986, 113). While feminist critics and scholars have undertaken, in recent years a wholesale house-cleaning, a gleeful debunking, of these harmful myths, the debilitating consequences of a history in which myth and culture have worked hand in hand to enfeeble women are still with us.

Women's deprivation of *mythos*, of *their* myth, and their cooptation or enslavement into the male mythic structures have reduced them to secondary creatures, deprived of their own voice. It is, therefore, especially in the area of expression—of the Book, that is, writing, literature—that the absence of their own myth has been particularly detrimental to women, since their access to the world of the Book has been effectively blocked by that negatively determining absence.

"Why, how, about what, where, when may I write?" asks the aspiring male writer, and myth answers him by proposing a distinguished genealogy and tradition of male creativity and authorship, beginning with Apollo, Orpheus, Homer, and continuing unbroken to the present. Into that prestigious genealogy a male author has only to insert himself, as in a lineage that is legitimately his. Although this insertion may well be accompanied by Oedipal pangs of anxiety, as Harold Bloom has demonstrated, and must be gained through a struggle against the predecessor/father, the precursor poet and text, it is nevertheless a project eminently, ritually, and empoweringly feasible for male authors, yet, based on an exclusively patriarchal model as it is, out of bounds for women. In the Oedipal conflict itself the seeds of the writer's eventual authority and power are embedded, but no such scheme is available to the woman writer. Sandra M. Gilbert and Susan Gubar, commenting on Bloom's formulation of the dynamic process that energizes Western literature, ask correctly: "Where, then, does the female poet fit in? . . . What if she can find no models, no precursors? Does she have a muse and what is its sex?" (1979, 47). They conclude that women do not "fit in," that, while men may experience an "anxiety of influence," would-be women writers feel "an even more primary 'anxiety of authorship'— a radical fear that she cannot create" (Gilbert and Gubar 1979, 49). To this very understandable, culturally dictated fear, there are no easy solutions and answers, yet women writers have always, through the centuries, attempted to find such answers, to grope towards solutions, to invent their own authority of origin, their own significant and empowering myths.

In the following pages, I explore the particular myths invented, out of need, desire, and frustration, by six different French women authors. Although the myths they formulate are different for each writer, their desire is the same in each case: to gain access to the Book.

The question of that access is of course particularly problematic for the four early women writers I have chosen: Marie de France (of the middle twelfth to the early thirteenth century), Madeleine and Catherine des Roches (respectively ca. 1520–87 and 1542–87), and

Marie de Gournay (1565–1645). I have selected these particular women because in their work I have seen most clearly evidence of coherent, if possibly unconscious, attempts to draw upon the mythic material of the past with which they were familiar, not to repeat and imitate it, but rather to refashion it in totally idiosyncratic ways into their own myth, a justification of themselves not only as writers, but as the particular kinds of writer they wanted to be. For Marie de France, the mythic material she refers to and exploits for her own precise ends is that of the Celtic past, whose enigmatic aura had just started to pervade Western literature when she began her writing project. She knew the classical myths, chiefly as retold by Ovid, but preferred the newer, wilder, less explored, less colonized material, as more apt to fit in, to be absorbed by, and expressive of, her own, new, "wild" project to be a woman writer. She uses that material to construct the myth of her own Celticity, as a validation of her marginality, and a way to gain access to writing.

Madeleine and Catherine des Roches remain faithful to their aspiration of gaining access to the Book—which for them means, inseparably, the intellectual realm of humanist learning so dominant in their period, and the poetic realm of writing—as humanist writers, that is, as scholar-authors, steeped in the Greek and Latin past and literature. As such, they refer for their mythic context to the forms, if not the identically reproduced substances of the classical myths. When they invent an original myth they couch it in terms reminiscent of the ancient mythic structures, but they endow it with a substance that is strikingly, rebelliously, new and daring: the proposal of an authentically female muse. This proposal includes a valorization of female bonding as indispensable to female creativity, and constitutes therefore a radical departure from patriarchal culture, in which, as Gilbert and Gubar remark, female bonding is "extraordinarily difficult" (1979, 38). Through this element of bonding, the Dames des Roches extend their mythic project for writing to all women, unlike Marie de France, who is so isolated as to seem completely ignorant of other women as writers—it is problematic enough to conceive of herself in that role[4]—and unlike Marie de Gournay.

Marie de Gournay's myth is defined as much by opposition as by desire. Her desire for the Book provoked a lifelong struggle against her own history, which did not destine her for learning and writing, and against her society, which resented her single-minded pursuit of writing as a profession, for it was very much that for her (though very incongruously, since she was a woman): a profession, a life, a livelihood in the spiritual as well as the economic sense of the word. For her mythic material, therefore, she turns, not surprisingly, away from her own century, using the death of her adopted father as an alibi: what age could be admirable that did not contain Montaigne? She turns to France's epic-heroic, mythical past and to Plato's Greece for mythopoeic material. She then adapts that material to the exact fit and shape of her need to surmount all obstacles thrown in her path, and to escape from the limitations her sex imposes on her. Here again, we have a completely idiosyncratic myth, tailor-made, as it were, by and for one woman writer, but nevertheless capable of inspiring others facing similar oppression and restriction.

Since my past scholarly work has mostly been in the area of the Middle Ages and the Renaissance, it is not surprising that I should have conceived of this book first in the context of these periods. My expertise has acquainted me with early writers, and I have long been impressed by the determination of the four I have chosen for this study to affirm their female voice, to write their female texts, despite obviously difficult historical/cultural contexts that did nothing to reassure or encourage them. Their valiant and challenging attempts to write themselves, that is, to write their own myths, have not necessarily resulted in prolonged acclaim and resounding success. While Marie de France is recognized as an important figure in French medieval literature, the Dames des Roches and Marie de Gournay, well known in their time, are today mostly forgotten, except by a handful of scholars and feminist critics. I agree, however, with Margaret Homans who, speaking about the nineteenth century women poets who are her subject, remarks that "they are as interesting for their failures as for their successes, because they show us the immensity of the difficulties to be confronted by any woman poet" (1980, 10). And, of course, I hope that this book will lead to a wider rediscovery and a new appreciation of these authors.

It is easily assumed that for contemporary women writers the earlier problems of access to the world of the Book have been abolished, and that anxiety of authorship is a thing of the past for them. The reading public, that curious, faceless amalgam, may easily believe that, for women today, writing lies as easily at hand as any other vocation. Of course, this is just another false myth; many vocations—and especially writing—remain difficult to attain for women. We are starting to perceive that women have not "made it" quite as far as we should like to think, and that the women who have seemingly succeeded have often done so at the cost of their authentic identity, their unique self, their "different voice," to use Carol Gilligan's expression. Those women, on the other hand, who have felt uneasy with surrender or compromise, or to whom resignation was simply unacceptable, have continued to reach toward the invention of their own unappropriated myth, as a repository of authority and creativity. As I read such post-World War II French authors as Simone de Beauvoir, Annie Leclerc, Christiane Rochefort, Colette Audry, Violette Leduc, Xavière Gauthier, Hélène Cixous, Monique Wittig, Benoîte Groult, Marguerite Duras, and others,[5] two things become overwhelmingly clear: first, very active, dynamic impulses are working toward demythification, toward the destruction of the old, stifling myths about women. This is not surprising, since this impulse coincides with the rise of international women's movements. The appearance and rapid advance of women's studies and feminist scholarship have contributed greatly to the activation and elaboration of that impulse in all fields of investigation: history, sociology, psychology, literature, to name just a few. In literary studies and philosophy, especially, the movement toward demythification has been aided significantly by the theories of Derridean deconstruction, and by feminist rereadings of Freud and Lacan.

Surprisingly, however, it is equally clear that a second, simultaneous, impulse towards remythification—that is, towards the continuing creation of specifically female empowering myths—is stronger and more articulate than ever. But, after all, the unprecedented sweeping away of the old, shopworn myths that has taken place in the second half of this century has liberated the female imagination as never before for the creation of her own myths, corresponding to her own purposes and to her continuing requirements and desires. It is obvious that the need for myth persists, as women continue to want to write on their own female terms.

As a consequence, the juxtaposition of early and contemporary writers may illuminate basic drives and strategies underlying much female writing. Myth making (or remaking) is clearly such a strategy. Mythopoeia is a method, as we have seen, of asking questions and producing answers. Women writers clearly continue to ask: "How is it possible to write?" and to provide answers out of the resources of their own rich unconscious, out of the experience of their own bodies, or by a deliberate reshaping, reversion, and revision, of male myths. In 1974, Xavière Gauthier wrote that "in French the word 'writer' does not have a feminine form" (Marks and de Courtivron 1980, 161).[6] Women are inventing new forms, new words, and finding in myths the force and the impetus to do so.

I have chosen Simone de Beauvoir and Hélène Cixous for this particular investigation for several reasons. The former stands at the beginning of this new myth making; the latter has profited already from the path-breaking work that has been done in France since Simone de Beauvoir published *The Second Sex* in 1949, by authors such as Monique Wittig, Christiane Rochefort, and Françoise Parturier, and by various women's study and action groups.[7] When Simone de Beauvoir began, as a young woman, to desire access to the Book, her immediate, primary, need was very precise: to be able to liberate herself from a suffocating milieu, to which ties of affection bound her while her aspirations called her to different, opposite, intellectual, ideological, and artistic worlds. For Cixous, that liberation was a more readily acquired fact, leaving her able to engage freely in the enterprise that interests her: a "defense and illustration" of female writing through the recuperation of old myths and through the invention of totally new mythic interpretations, creations, and syntheses. Simone de Beauvoir's mythic structures are exemplary for other women, but spring primarily from her unconscious need to justify the necessary but painful break with a cherished/despised environment. Cixous extends her invitation to myth making, which she sees as inseparable from access to writing, to all women. Adopting the stance of a visionary and an apostle, she reconciles the mythic enterprise *in toto* with the elaboration of an inclusive model of female existence and writing. Through their separate uses of myth, these two modern writers add individual dimensions to those created by the four early writers, yet the same underlying needs and desires are present in the writing of all six.

But there is another, personal, reason for my choice of Simone de Beauvoir and Hélène Cixous as well: my initial encounters with the writing of both women were accompanied by subjective experiences deepening my response.

When I first read Simone de Beauvoir as an adolescent, I, like many women of my generation, was strongly marked by the hopeful revelations she offered women in *The Second Sex:* that women need not be merely what they had for so long seemed destined to be, that is, secondary, submissive, restricted creatures; that immense worlds of possibilities were accessible to women, too; that woman could take her life and work in her own hands, and gain self-worth through self-affirmation. Many of Beauvoir's ideas may seem obvious now, but they were not when we first read them in the late forties and early fifties, and when I read Simone de Beauvoir with undergraduates today I still see the force of revelation or re-revelation at work. But as much as her writings, it was the manifestation of an exemplary personality that impressed me in Simone de Beauvoir. Here was somebody from a milieu very much like my own, educated in a very similar way, with the same values, the same readings, the same "culture," who had been able to transcend that milieu to become the author not only of her own life but of her own texts, fully aware of the difficulties that "escape," as she calls it in the introduction to *The Second Sex*, entailed and continues to entail for women who want to follow her example.

Hélène Cixous's works, which I encountered almost thirty years later, are obviously very different, yet I heard in them the same persuasive, blessedly opinionated, strong voice I had heard in the writing of Simone de Beauvoir. On first reading "The Laugh of the Medusa" it seemed impossible not to be exhilarated by her lyrical, urgent discourse, impelling women toward writing, proposing her own example, at the end of the piece, as a model of female expression, in a typical alliance of the authorly "I" and the female "we" in a joint undertaking: "When I write, it's everything that we don't know we can be that is written out of me, without exclusions, without stipulation, and everything we will be calls us to the unflagging, intoxicating, unappeasable search for love. In one another we will never be lacking" (Cixous 1976, 893).

For each of the five female voices (representing six writers, including the collaboration of Madeleine and Catherine des Roches) treated in this book, I have chosen one particular work in which I see most clearly the formulation of the desire for writing, and of the mythic construct each invents to gain access to that world of the Book. The choice was always self-evident, except in the case of Hélène Cixous, since almost all of her writing is imbued with the mythic impulse. The work I chose, *Illa*, is, however, particularly illustrative, in its imagery and in its use of the Ceres-Proserpina myth, of traits that will have been already observed in the texts of the previously treated authors.

An appropriate bibliographical list follows each of the five chapters, since each one, while thematically connected with the others, treats also a distinct and discrete subject. There is a certain overlap between the bibliographies, however, which signifies that certain critics have guided me throughout this book.

The translations of all quotes from the six authors in question, as well as from the critics and scholars I cite, are by me, unless otherwise indicated in the notes or the bibliography.

Notes

1. The translation is by Albert Cook. These words of Telemachus to Penelope are repeated almost identically—except for one word—in a later book of the *Odyssey* (21: 350–53), when the son says to his mother: "Go into the house and attend to your own tasks,/ The loom and the distaff, and give orders to your servants/ To set at the work. The *bow* shall concern all the men/ But me especially. For the power in the house is mine." Like speech, the bow—which replaces it in this passage, and signifies male activity—is forbidden to women, who, as they are relegated to domesticity, are deprived of meaningful action *and* of expression, since these are seen as quasi-identical: one replaces the other smoothly in Telemachus's admonitions to Penelope.

2. The earlier lines from the Demeny letter were translated by me, but this last quote was taken from H. M. Parshley's translation of a text by Simone de Beauvoir, in which Beauvoir cites these well-known words of Rimbaud (Marks and de Courtivron, 1980, 233).

3. The genre of the *blasons* knew a great success among the poets of the French Renaissance. It consisted in descriptions of an abstraction, an object, but most frequently of a part of the female body, with a great deal of attention paid to detail and piquancy.

4. As Peter Dronke has shown, a considerable number of women writers were active throughout the Middle Ages. However, in Marie de France's Anglo-Norman world, few women were writing, as she did, in the vernacular. She may have known of the *trobairitz* of Provence who composed in Provençal, but no traces of that possible acquaintance are found in her work.

5. Many of these writers have been excerpted in the anthology by Elaine Marks and Isabelle de Courtivron, which serves as an invaluable introduction to recent writing by French women.

6. In French dictionaries, the word *écrivaine* does not exist, but the term is beginning to be used by women; in fact, it is already commonly found in Canada.

7. For an overview of French feminism since the Middle Ages, and of the new French feminist expressions and manifestations, see Marks's introduction.

Works Cited in and Consulted for the Introduction

Beauvoir, Simone de. 1949. *Le Deuxième Sexe*. 2 vols. Paris: Gallimard.

Bloom, Harold. 1973. *The Anxiety of Influence: A Theory of Poetry*. New York: Oxford University Press.

Cixous, Hélène. 1976. "The Laugh of the Medusa." Trans. Keith Cohen and Paula Cohen. *Signs* 1:875–93.

Cook, Albert, trans. 1967. *The Odyssey: A New Verse Translation*. New York: W. W. Norton.

———. 1980. *Myth and Language*. Bloomington: Indiana University Press.

Daly, Mary. 1978. *Gyn/Ecology: The Metaethics of Radical Feminism*. Boston: Beacon Press.

Delany, Sheila. 1983. *Writing Woman: Women Writers and Women in Literature Medieval to Modern*. New York: Schocken Books.

Dove, Rita. 1986. "Two Poems." *TriQuarterly* 67:113–14.

Dronke, Peter. 1984. *Women Writers of the Middle Ages*. Cambridge: Cambridge University Press.

Ellman, Mary. 1968. *Thinking About Women*. New York: Harcourt Brace Jovanovich.

Gilbert, Sandra M., and Susan Gubar. 1979. *The Madwoman in the Attic: The Woman Writer and the Nineteenth Century Literary Imagination*. New Haven: Yale University Press.

Gilligan, Carol. 1982. *In a Different Voice*. Cambridge: Harvard University Press.

Heilbrun, Carolyn G. 1979. *Reinventing Womanhood*. New York: W. W. Norton.

Homans, Margaret. 1980. *Women Writers and Poetic Identity*. Princeton: Princeton University Press.

Jolles, André. 1965. *Einfache Formen*. Tübingen: Max Niemeyer Verlag.

Lipking, Lawrence. 1983. "Aristotle's Sister: A Poetics of Abandonment." *Critical Inquiry* 10:61–81.

Marks, Elaine, and Isabelle de Courtivron. 1980. *New French Feminisms: An Anthology*. Amherst: University of Massachusetts Press.

Olsen, Tillie. 1978. *Silences*. New York: Delacorte Press/Seymour Lawrence.

Rich, Adrienne. 1975. *Poems Selected and New, 1950–1974*. New York: W. W. Norton.

———. 1979. *On Lies, Secrets, and Silence*. New York: W. W. Norton.

———. 1981. *A Wild Patience Has Taken Me This Far: Poems 1978–1981*. New York: W. W. Norton.

Rimbaud, Arthur. (1871) 1981. *Œuvres*. Paris: Garnier.

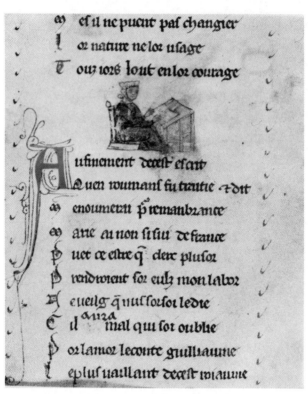

Illustration of Marie de France's *Les Fables d'Ysopet*. Thirteenth century. Reprinted by courtesy of the Bibliothèque Nationale, Paris.

⫷ 1 ⫸
ℳarie de France
The Myth of the Wild

Wild is the name of the Self in women . . .

Mary Daly

Marie de France is one of the best examples of that tantalizing and typically medieval figure, the well-known author about whom almost nothing is known. She may be called today "the first woman novelist of our era" (Fowles 1978, ix), and "perhaps the greatest woman author of the Middle Ages" (Hanning and Ferrante 1978, 1), but her identity remains mysterious, albeit the subject of much research and speculation.

Three works, all dated within the latter part of the twelfth century and the beginning of the thirteenth, are signed with the name Marie. In one, a collection of fables translated from English into French, we read in the first lines of the epilog this statement: "At the end of this work, which I have translated into French, I'll name myself for memory's sake: my name is Marie, and I am from France." The author then adds: "It is possible that some clerks might take my book for themselves. I do not wish anyone to claim it, for she who lets herself be forgotten does bad work," thus giving us, not only her name, but a strong sense of the importance she attaches to recognition of her authorship and to literary survival.

In another work, a translation into French from the Latin text *Tractatus de Purgatorio Sancti Patricii,* "Saint Patrick's Purgatory," we read in the first lines of the brief epilog, "I, Marie, have preserved for

15

posterity the book about Purgatory, in French, so that it may be understood by and accessible to the lay person."

Finally we look at yet a third work, which may have been written between the other two.[1] This is a collection of twelve narrative *lais*, or rhymed stories, contained in a British Museum manuscript of the mid-thirteenth century (Burgess 1977). In the prologue to the first *lai*, entitled "Guigemar" we read: "Whoever deals with good material is very disturbed when the work is not done well. Listen, Lords, to what Marie has to say, who, in her time [i.e., when it is her turn to write] does not let herself be forgotten."

Three times the name Marie, three times the notion of the importance of not being forgotten! And we have yet another witness to the existence of a writer named Marie. In a book entitled *La Vie Seint Edmund le rei* ("The life of Saint Edmund the king"), placed at the end of the twelfth century and probably composed by a monk called Denis Piramus, we find mention of a "Lady Marie who wrote in rhyme and composed the verses of *lais* which are not at all true. And so is she much praised because of it, and the rhymes loved everywhere."[2]

Four times Marie then! Are they all one and the same person? And, if so, who is that person? To the first question I believe that we may answer yes (although not all scholars would agree), if we accept Emanuel Mickel's argument that, "given the fact that women writers were not exactly commonplace, is it likely that there were four different women all with the name Marie, composing texts in the late twelfth and early thirteenth century?" (1974, 15); women writers, we may add, with the same interest in naming themselves, and in expressing their interest in a lasting reputation.

To the second question the answer remains unclear. Various suggestions have been offered—from a Marie, natural daughter of Geoffrey Plantagenet and abbess of Shaftesbury, to a nun at the abbey of Reading—but it is impossible to make a positive identification. We may say that Marie was, in all likelihood, a native of France, probably of Ile-de-France or Normandy, who spent a good part of her life in England, in aristocratic and maybe monastic circles. She was obviously well-educated, which indicates a high birth, since she knew Latin as well as French and English, and was well versed in literature, ancient and contemporary, as allusions and borrowings in her work allow us to conclude.

As a woman writer[3] she is certainly a rarity in her Anglo-Norman milieu: a bird of a different feather! As we have already noted, she counters that gender-situated difference, which sets her apart, with a strong refusal to let it exclude her from her chosen sphere of literary activity, and from recognition for that activity. The fact that she states her name so emphatically, affirms her claims on her work against possible usurpers with such conviction, and insists on the importance of not being forgotten, signifies an assumption of difference as well as a sense and affirmation of identity.

The *Lais*, Marie de France's most important work, comprises a collection of twelve narrative poems,[4] the longest having 1,184 octo-syllabic lines and the shortest having 118. Each tells a story about a different modality of love, from the egocentric and destructive to the self-forgetting and redemptive; from the cruel and rapacious to the courtly and refined; from the painfully suffering to the joyfully liberating. John Fowles talks about Marie's "characteristic obsession with the problems of sexuality and fidelity" (1978, xi) and compares her with Jane Austen, in that "she set a new standard for accuracy over human emotions and their absurdity" (1974, 106). Although it has by now become a commonplace to compare early women writers, or any women writers showing interest in psychology, with Jane Austen, Fowles is right to stress Marie's fascinated observation and evocation, in all her stories, of human sexual and social behaviour. The collection is preceded by a prologue which, scholars speculate, was written after the completion of the work, since, as we have seen, the first *lai*, "Guigemar," also starts with a general introduction in which Marie names herself "at the beginning of my enterprise" (line 22).[5] It is very likely that a more extensive, more elaborate prologue, containing an aesthetic program with precise remarks concerning the nature and contents of the texts, and a statement about the author's intentions, would be delayed until the very task of composition had allowed Marie to understand more clearly her own interests and motivation and to gain both a more comprehensive insight into her work and an overview of her accomplishment and of the characteristics setting it apart from the writings of her contemporaries.

She to whom God has given knowledge
And good eloquence in speech,

Should not be silent or secretive about these gifts,
But should show them willingly.
When a great good is much talked about,   5
Then it may start to bloom,
And when many people praise it,
Then it has spread its flowers.
It was the custom among the ancient writers,
As Priscian testifies,   10
That, in the books they composed,
They spoke obscurely,
So that those who came after them
And who would study them
Were able to explicate their words   15
And to provide them with the complete meaning.
The wise old writers knew this,
For they understood, from their own experience,
That, as time passed,
Readers would become more subtle in their intelligence,   20
And would be more able to guard themselves
From possible errors in interpretation.
She who wishes to defend herself from vice
Must study and understand,
And begin a difficult work.   25
Through that effort one may distance
And deliver oneself from great pain.
That is why I first started to think
About composing some good stories
And about translating from Latin into French.   30
But that would not bring me any fame,
So many others have done it!
Then I thought of the *lais* which I had heard.
I did not doubt, I knew well,
That for memory's sake they composed them   35
From adventures they had heard about,
Those who first began them
And who sent them forth into the world.
I have heard many of them told,
And I do not want to forget or neglect them.   40
I have put them into rhyme, and have made them into a
    poetic work.
Often to do this, I have stayed up all night!
In your honor, noble King,
Who are so valiant and courteous,
Whom all joy salutes,   45

And in whose heart all good takes root,
I undertook to assemble these *Lais*,
To provide them with rhyme and to retell them.
In my heart I thought and decided,
Sire, that I would present them to you.   50
If it pleases you to receive them
You will cause me great joy,
Forever shall I be gladdened!
Do not think me presumptuous
If I dare give you this present.   55
Now listen to the beginning.

This Prolog has been widely studied as the interesting literary document it is.[6] Foulet and Uitti correctly detect in this text two important concepts: "the sovereign importance of dynamic tradition (translatio studii) and the equally vital [one] of literary legitimacy" (1981, 248). As these scholars point out, the two concepts are inseparable for Marie, as they would be for most medieval authors, as the belonging to a chain of tradition also justifies the present, new work, and allows its authors to undertake it with a certain measure of authorial self-confidence. Marie, as a woman writer, must be doubly anxious to establish the legitimacy of her enterprise.

She sets out by stating, in lines 1–8, a justification for writing which rests on the "do not hide your light under a bushel" argument. As a female author she may have felt that pious alibi to be especially useful. The beginning lines of the first *lai*, "Guigemar," help to explain further a certain note of defensiveness we detect in her self-justification: "People should praise those/ Who cause others to speak well of them./ But when there is somewhere/ A man or a woman of great worth/ Those who are jealous of them/ Often say vile things about them,/ For they want to diminish their reputation./ And so they act the role of evil, cowardly, vicious dogs/ Who bite people treacherously./ I do not want to give up because of that./ If sneerers and backbiters/ Wish to turn my determination against me/ It is their right to speak evil" (lines 5–18).

Marie clearly addresses herself here to those who have criticized her for a previous excursion into the world of literature, probably the translation of the *Fables*. Surely the criticism—and it must have been savage to warrant such a lengthy, bitter, and defiant reply at the start of Marie's new work—cannot have been aimed at her subject matter, for the genre of the Aesopic fable was a popular one in the Middle Ages (Lenaghan 1967, Introduction), unobjectionable to the feudal and courtly milieu. When a woman chose to practice it, however, it may have appeared not quite seemly either that she should "retain the scatological or obscene language attributed to birds and beasts who figure in the fables" (Malvern 1983, 29), or that she should use her strong authorial voice to formulate some of the rather bold and maybe too pointed lessons concluding each piece. We may, then, speculate that the criticisms and attacks were aimed at Marie's femaleness, and thus at her transgression of the limits within which women were allowed to participate in courtly literature, namely as admired objects, as members of a delighted and delightful public, or as beneficient patrons.

In the opening lines of the Prolog, Marie has toned down, or even hidden, the resentment she felt and had expressed in "Guigemar," and, ostensibly ignoring the inflicted hurt, stresses that she wishes to write as an act of obedience to Christ's commandment, implied in the parable recounted by Matthew (25:14–30), that one should not bury one's talents, but exploit and multiply them, lest one be cast out as useless and undeserving.

She then links herself to a recognized literary lineage through the mention (lines 9–22) of the sixth-century grammarian Priscian, whose *Institutio grammatica* may well have been her own textbook for the study of Latin. This work, containing, as it does, copious examples from classical authors, provided an education in literature as well as language (Curtius 1948, 43), and thus an introduction to well-established traditions of writing, reading, and interpretation as continuous processes of literary production and study. In lines 23–27, we see a second, more focused and personalized justification for writing: that it helps to free one from vice and pain. Foulet and Uitti make the interesting suggestion that this is an allusion to accidie (1981, 247). In John Cassian's influential fifth-century list of sins—of which he names eight—*acedia* is defined as "anxietas sive taedium cordis." Gregory the Great, a century and a half later, merges *tristitia* with *acedia* under the former name, which is significant for the perception of the latter as a state of spiritual discouragement and prostration. Saint Thomas Aquinas equally preferred the name *tristitia* defining it as an emptiness of the soul. However, it is *acedia* which was eventually retained. At first of interest mainly in theological literature, the sins began to be treated more and more often by secular writers also, with certain changes of meaning taking place. So *acedia*, or *accidia*, gradually lost its spiritual connotations of despair, deep melancholy, and dryness of spirit, and came to be seen increasingly, in the later Middle Ages, as a synonym for sloth (Bloomfield 1967, 72). By the twelfth century, the spiritual sense of metaphysical despair and *taedium* was still very much present both in Latin and in vernacular theological literature, and Marie de France, in all likelihood, transposed a primarily religious concept to her own spiritual, albeit secular, experience. A state of metaphysical despair then becomes a state of sadness, discouragement, and anxiety, which might well assail a woman sure of her gifts ("knowledge . . . eloquence in speech") but not necessarily sure of the acceptability and possibility of bringing these gifts to full flowering. In this connection, Joan Ferrante speaks about Marie's "frustration as an intelligent and gifted woman with few outlets for her skill in the secular world" (1984, 67). The idea of particular virtues as remedies for particular sins was commonplace in the Middle Ages, and the remedial virtue for *acedia* was the virtue of strength—in Marie's case the strength to undertake the first preliminary work of study and understanding, and then the difficult, arduous task of writing that she mentions in lines 24 and 25.

In lines 28–42, she speaks in very direct terms about her own work, explaining how she made the decisions of what to do and what options to reject. Again, we are in the presence of a self-valorizing author, who is not afraid to say no to her contemporaries' Latin inspiration, and who deliberately chooses another direction, that of the Celtic story material evoked here by the word *lais*, and by the memory of their long-ago composers. As Michelle Freeman has remarked in talking about the Prolog, Marie is very "preoccupied with origins" and "chooses to distinguish herself . . . by locating a new point of origin" (1984, 860, 883). In doing this she deliberately transfers her "difference" from her biological and social experience to her artistic purpose and accomplishment. The statement, "I have put them [i.e., the Celtic materials] into rhyme, and have made them into a poetic work" (line 41), and the proud reminder of the difficulty of the undertaking, which has caused her many sleepless nights, underline, again, the solemnity and assurance of her authorly stance. From the defensiveness of the beginning of the Prolog she has moved to confidence. Foulet and Uitti remark that "she is narrating, so to speak, a chapter of her own life, in a text that abounds in first person verbs" (1981, 248). Indeed, the Prolog may be seen as a journey from initial insecurity to an assurance acquired in the foothold of tradition, and then to an assurance and individuality grounded in reclaimed, almost defiant, difference.

Is this a typically female itinerary? There is no such thing as typicality when we speak of medieval women writers, but we may see, in Marie's self-described evolution, first the traces of female tentativeness and then the eventual female revindication of otherness. Condemned to be other, she finally chooses to be. The "narration" of herself is the subtext of the entire Prolog, her "how I came to be a writer," and we read of her career as one fraught with doubt at the outset, yet from the outset benefiting from the assets of a strong, even rebellious, fighting personality. In his book on poetic careers, Lawrence Lipking notes about Homer that "he lived first in his own imagination and eventually in ours" (1981, 11). Marie de France, as all poets must, follows that same trajectory, but to be born as a writer in her own imagination requires an extra revelation, seconded by effort and will, in the case of an early woman author who has few precedents and no or few models. To imagine herself as a writer and to imagine her work must have been much more difficult for Marie than for any of her male contemporaries. In the Prolog, she traces her steady and obstinate implementation of that initial imagining. Nor does she neglect the second term indicated by Lipking: through her constant preoccupation with memory and remembrance we see her projecting herself into the imagination of future readers. Her dedication of the *Lais* is addressed in lines 43–56 to Henry II (Mickel 1974, 19), but beyond him to all readers, and the joy she anticipates (lines 52–53) is the joy of the "life of the poet."

In the Prolog, then, Marie performs a double act: of assimilation, by linking herself to an existing and respected tradition, and of differentiation, by choosing Celtic subject matter for her work. Indeed, we may say that that choice is the culmination of a process of differentiation—within assimilation—which began when she signed her *Fables*, saying "my name is Marie."

In all her *lais*, as well as in the Prolog, Marie de France alludes to an earlier tradition, invariably oral and invariably Breton (i.e., Celtic),[7] which she presents as the indispensable inspiration for and the basic material of her own literary work. In the short prologue to "Guigemar," she states the Celticity of her inspiration for all her *lais*, and in each subsequent *lai*, she reaffirms this. The only exception is "Chievrefoil"; since the story takes as its theme and content the already well-known tale of Tristan and Isolde, it would be clear to any public that this is a Celtic legend. In all the other *lais,* Marie either states in the opening lines that "the Bretons composed a *lai* about it," or specifically names many of her characters and settings as Breton; sometimes we find both at the same time: affirmation of a Celtic source and of the Celticity of the *dramatis personae* and *loci.* But, as many critics have noticed, while Marie calls all her themes Breton, "the majority of the *lais* have nothing particularly Celtic about them" (Mickel 59), and in the very rare cases where Celtic lore is present "she did not understand the motifs in reference to the mythology from which they derived nor does her combination of motifs have meaning in terms of Celtic lore" (Mickel 1974, 67).

It has been suggested that she was mostly concerned with providing her public with settings that had become newly fashionable through the popularity of Geoffroy of Monmouth's *Historia Regum Britanniae* (ca. 1135), a fictional history of Great Britain based on Arthurian legend, and of its adaptation into French verse, Wace's *Brut* (1155). But this does not explain adequately or satisfactorily the persistence with which Marie reiterates her ties with an oral Breton past. By restating these bonds in slightly different ways in each *lai,* she simultaneously explores them and she integrates them effectively into her work.

Freeman has a much more interesting idea when she suggests that Marie's choice "of at least nominally Celtic but non-Arthurian material over Roman or French might well reflect in itself a mode of feminizing what may be considered appropriate material for a new *translatio studii;* namely the literature of that class (or race) of people— the Britons—delivered from one oppressor (the Saxons) and protected by another more benevolent but nevertheless dominant class (the Normans)" (1984, 879 n. 8). This idea is much more interesting because it places Marie's claimed Celticity, not in an exterior circumstance such as literary or courtly fashion, but in the interiority of Marie's unconventional impulse towards writing, and, specifically, in Marie's female desire of authorship. Freeman sees Marie, then, as aligning herself with settings, plots, and characters "not entailed in a noteworthy patriarchal lineage."

While it is evident that Marie intends to pursue difference, and that her pursuit leads her away from the patriarchal structures of her society and of its literature, it is less evident that in doing so, as Freeman suggests, Marie sees that difference as connected with weakness and need for protection and considers the Celts, her source of difference, as an oppressed, even when kindly patronized, race. For the oppression-submission model presented by Freeman to describe Celticity/femaleness, we may substitute a model of repression countered by expression. Like the Celtic voice, the female voice refuses repression and speaks. For Marie de France, the Breton territory *of her own making* is not one of oppression, it is a free zone, where neither Saxon nor Norman has ever trodden, in other words, a wild, uncultivated zone.

This notion of a wild zone, of an area of wildness, is not a fanciful or fantastic one. It is the interiorization of a geographic and social phenomenon of the period: the existence of marginal beings, and of unpopulated, uncultivated spaces (Le Goff 1964, 169ff., 387 ff.). Both figure abundantly in the literature and the iconography of the period (Husband 1980), and correspond to the marginal or excluded creatures—lepers, beggars, madmen, hermits—dwelling on the edges of or well outside an increasingly structured social order, and to the vast uninhabited spaces—forests, wastelands, marshes—surrounding the villages, castles, and towns, and bordering the cultivated fields of an increasingly expanding agriculture. More importantly, both wild men and wild spaces correspond to the interior wildness that medieval man observes in himself and in his society, and that he sees as a menace to a precarious moral and emotional equilibrium in himself and in the civilization in which he lives, but they also serve as a valorization of that wildness, perceived in this sense not as a threat but as a salutary means of escape from an increasingly regularized society. As Husband says: "Sublimated in the wild man were the permanent phobias of medieval society—chaos, insanity, and ungodliness" (1980, 5), but on the other hand, "the wild man's disassociation from . . . the institutions from which he had been barred . . . placed him in a positive light" (1980, 15), as he now "held up before man the possibilities of a free existence if he broke the shackles convention placed upon him" (1980, 17).

It is this latter aspect of wildness—the freedom from conventionality—that Marie de France is able to locate in the Celtic material, or rather in the myth she constructed of that Celticity, for she is not at all concerned, as we have seen, with an authentic, coherent rendering of Celtic lore. If she is an archaeologist, it is not of a historical Celticity, but of a Celticity of the mind and the imagination. She may very well have heard old Celtic legends told at the court where she resided, and she was obviously familiar with the existence of an old Celtic culture, but it is not the recreation of that culture which concerns her, but rather the fact—which she will make her own—of its enigmatic and therefore still totally imaginable (rather than discoverable) existence. She endows both Celticity and orality with an aura of formlessness, freedom, and freshness, which she sees as attractive and fertile qualities for the very foundation of her writing: guarantees of newness and originality, of difference—her own much stressed difference. Has she not rejected the *translatio* of Latin subjects as trite and unoriginal? By claiming oral and Breton roots for her writing she is able to posit for herself the mythical existence of a unified, solid substratum, parallel but superior to the rejected Latin one, for her *Lais*. At the same time, she retains the freedom both to create that substratum according to her tastes and needs, her imagination and her own "wildness," and fashion the literary work in accordance with her interest in form, order, and the classical tradition. The Celticity/ orality construct serves as an expression of her otherness, and as a guarantee of her authorial freedom, but she does not want to break with tradition, as she has made clear in the Prolog. One offers the pleasure of the exhilaratingly formless, the other the joy of meaningful form giving. One corresponds to an uncharted "female" domain (since the territory of authorship was indeed largely new to women, exceptions notwithstanding), the other to a clearly mapped-out "male" domain. Thus she may continue to affirm her own different poetic identity while also claiming her place in the established tradition.

The anthropologist Edwin Ardener offers a model of society in which men and women interact in certain areas and are separate in others, as one of intersecting and thus partially coinciding circles. The section, or crescent, of the women's circle falling outside the men's area constitutes the women's "wild" zone. In comparison to the dominant male one it is a muted zone, which Ardener describes further in this way: "Where society is defined by men, some features of women do not fit that definition. In rural societies, the anomaly is experienced as a feature of the 'wild,' for the 'wild' is a metaphor of the non-social" (Ardener 1975, 23). Elaine Showalter, applying Ardener's model to women writers, states that "women writing are not then, *inside* and *outside* of the male tradition; they are inside two traditions simultaneously" (1985, 264), a formulation that captures Marie's determination to belong to the male world of conventional

literature while implanting in that world her female sphere of unconventional wildness. She wants to belong to the reality of writing as a
public and social act while preserving her identity and her difference
through the myth of a unified and unique inspiration emerging from
the wilds of Celticity, to be captured by her as the unicorn was captured by the maiden. Her next work, after the *Lais*, is a translation
from Latin: obviously she does not disdain that exercise and the tradition it perpetuates, but she does want to explore also another writing practice, one that would give a strong voice to her difference. In
order to go beyond *translatio*—the perception of herself as a vessel
through which a culture passes—she must go on to *inventio*, and the
perception of herself as a cultivator of new ground, a discoverer of
new fields. This new area must be at the same time idiosyncratic
(wholly hers) and unified (whole). Although, as many scholars have
pointed out, a variety of thematic elements are detectable in the work
of Marie de France, not least numerous references to Ovidian
themes, Marie does not admit to a concatenation of different sources
for her work, but insists on a unified origin.

From tradition she wants the security of belonging to the literary establishment, the availability of form and discipline, and the
assured access to posterity; from her self-created myth she wants
continued access to the authenticity of her own inspiration and imagination, and a justification of her difference. In order to reach both
objectives she organizes a close parallel between tradition and myth.
Both are whole; both are old; both are connected with the notion of
remembrance, that is, survival. Into that parallel she then introduces
an element of divergence: where the tradition is Latin and written,
the myth is Celtic and oral. Through the integration of the myth
into the comparative scheme, and then its partial deviation from
that scheme, she renders acceptable both her partial adherence to
tradition and her partial rejection of it. She obliterates a possible
marginality-as-exclusion, and replaces it with marginality-as-
distinction. The myth of the oral Celticity of her material transfers an
extension of the fact of Marie's difference and wildness (as a woman
writer) from the body of her female-ness onto that of her writer-ness,
resulting in a fertilization of that difference that allows it to bear fruit
in the *Lais*. The notion of wildness allied to difference is inseparable
from the *Lais'* genesis, but Marie de France also uses it, within the
macrocosmic space of the total work, to sow microcosmic indications
and clues to the value and redemptiveness of the notion.

The following remarks are not meant to offer a complete interpretation of the *Lais*, but to underline a few examples of wildness-as-good in the work, and to show that these instances are never arbitrary embellishments, pleasant but inconsequential, but serve instead to advance the plot, to evoke the emotions or qualities of the protagonists—doubt, hesitation, ambivalence, love, desire, goodness—and to suggest positive solutions to problematic situations.

In "Guigemar," the wild spaces of the forest and the sea serve to make possible the hero's voyage towards eventual maturity and self-realization. It is in the forest that Guigemar receives the wound that forces him to change his immature ways and to search for healing; it is on the sea that he is carried to the different phases of his destiny.

In "Fresne," the heroine, the embodiment of selfless love, born in a courtly milieu, is transformed into a "wild" child when her mother casts her off, and she is left as a foundling, without name or social identity, in an ash tree. Educated by a charitable abbess, she becomes a young woman "noble of character and of good learning" (line 239) as well as courtly and beautiful, but it is her unquestioning and uncomplaining acceptance of her marginality (she may be loved but not wed by a knight) that eventually allows her not only to recover her identity and rank in society (with the noble marriage as a happy result), but also to effect the spiritual salvation of her mother.

In "Bisclavret," the coexistence in one character of wildness and goodness is even more remarkable, since the wildness takes here the shape of utmost marginality: that of the werewolf. But while the man-beast, even when hunted in the woods, is capable of gentleness and intelligence ("This beast . . . has the mind of a man," remarks the king who encounters Bisclavret, "this beast has understanding and sense"), his fully "human" wife is cruel, disloyal, and deceitful. It is Bisclavret who causes his wife to be brought to justice, and to be sent, defaced and debased, into exile, so that she now becomes a marginalized and monstrous creature, unredeemed and cast out, while he becomes reintegrated into the courtly society he has purified of an evil and illegal presence.

In "Lanval," the hero's mysterious, enigmatic lover takes him away from the court of King Arthur, where he had suffered injustice and persecution, and brings him to the beautiful island of Avalon, a free and wild space into which they disappear forever.

In "Les Deus Amanz," the flowering of the wild mountainside redeems the tragic but rather foolish love of the two young protagonists, and the story ends with the vista of their marble tomb, desolate sign of futile death, on a mountain summit aromatic with "many good herbs" (line 228), consoling sign of fertile life.

The nightingale of "Laüstic" and the hawk-knight of "Yonec" are both wild creatures signifying the joy and yearning of love. Both are painfully destroyed by a husband's jealous rage; both leave behind a legacy. In the tale, "Yonec," this legacy takes the form of a son, Yonec, "handsome, good, and brave" (line 461), who avenges his father's death and his mother's suffering. In "Laüstic," the small corpse of the wild bird is wrapped by the lady "in a piece of samite, covered in gold-embroidered writing" (lines 135–36). This "writing"—the message the lady sends to her lover to inform him of the enforced end of their platonic meetings which the nightingale's song had alibied—is a typically female text, akin to the one Philomela sent to her sister Procne in the form of a tapestry into which she has woven the terrible story of her violation, mutilation, and imprisonment by Procne's husband, Tereus.[8] The lover has the little corpse sealed in a precious gold casket encrusted with jewels, "which he carried with him always" (line 156). The wild creature, whose voice, as the woman's, has been stilled, finds survival in remembrance.

More wild creatures are found in "Milun," where the swan serves love's purpose, and in "Eliduc," where the weasel gives a Christ-like example of life-restoring, redemptive love, which triumphs, radiantly, at the end of the tale.

In two *lais*, "Equitan" and "Chaitivel," there are neither wild creatures nor wild spaces (except for a brief allusion to hunting in the former), and both are stories of destruction, "Equitan" concerning unremitting disloyalty and cruelty and "Chaitivel," destructive, shallow love-games. At the end of "Chaitivel," the frivolous lady who has caused the death of three of her four lovers and the lasting unhappiness of the fourth, decides to compose a *lai* about them. Redemption of great pain and sorrow through artistic creation? It might have been, but it is not. As Mickel points out, "Even here [in proposing the composition] the woman's gross selfishness is apparent in her emphasis on her own misery and what she had lost" (1974, 117), and Marie de France seems to indicate that this self-absorption and banal egocentrism cannot find resonances beyond its own narcissistic preoccupations: in the three last lines of the *lai*, she seems to seal the subject off once and for all: "here it is ended, there is no more, I have heard no more, and I know no more, and I shall tell you no more about it."

The *lai* of "Chievrefoil" is the total opposite of "Chaitivel." Here too we encounter love and suffering, here too the story ends with the composition of a *lai*, but here the love is fertile and creative, and the act of literary composition is one of enormous resonance and richness. "Chievrefoil" (Honeysuckle) deserves a separate and more detailed treatment, for in this *lai* Marie de France uses the Celtic material of the Tristan and Isolde legend to invent an entirely new episode for the already famous story (Mickel 1974, 94 and 95) and to explore, through her invention, her own central concerns: the links between tradition and individuality, between civilization and wildness, between convention and freedom. In this, the shortest of her *lais*, she offers in an admirably concise and eloquent form all the essential elements of the Tristan and Isolde myth, summed up in the episode's central metaphor of the honeysuckle and the hazel tree, which expresses the dual notions of attachment (equaling life) and separation (equaling death) underlying the celebrated love story:

It pleases me and I wish
To tell you the truth
Of the *lai* called "Chievrefoil,"
Why and how it was composed, and where it came from.
Many have told and recited it to me,   5
And I have composed it in writing,
About Tristan and the Queen,
About their love which was so true
And caused them so much sorrow,
Until they died of it the same day.   10
King Mark was irritated,
Angry with his nephew Tristan;
He exiled him from his land
Because of the Queen whom he loved.
Tristan went into his own country,   15
South Wales, where he was born.
He stayed there a whole year,
For he could not come back.
Ever more he abandoned himself
To death and destruction.   20
That should not surprise you,
For one who loves faithfully
Is very sad and troubled
When his desires are not fulfilled.
Tristan was sad and troubled,   25

So he left his country
And went straight to Cornwall
Where the Queen lived.
He went into the forest all alone,
For he did not want to be seen by anybody.   30
In the evening he came out,
When it was time to look for shelter.
With peasants, with poor people,
He found lodging for the night.
He asked them for news   35
About the King, about how he was.
They told him that they had heard
That the barons were all called by convocation
To come to Tintagel
Where the King wanted to hold his court.   40
At Pentecost they would all be there,
And there would be much joy and pleasure,
And the Queen would be there too.
Tristan heard that, and was very glad,
For she would not be able to go there   45
Without him seeing her pass by.
The day the King started out
Tristan returned into the woods.
On the road where he knew
The cortege must pass   50
He cut a hazel tree in half,
Split and squared it.
When he had so prepared the wood
He wrote his name on it with his knife.
If the Queen noticed it,   55
Who would be carefully watching out for it
(For it had happened once before,
And she had noticed it then),
She would certainly recognize her lover's
Stick of wood when she saw it.   60
It was the gist of the letter
He had sent her, in which he had said
That he had been there a long time,
That he had waited and kept quiet
In order to discover and to know   65
How he could see her,
For he could not live without her.
With the two of them it was just
As it is with the honeysuckle

Who clings to the hazel tree.   70
When it has wound itself around it and embraced
And enveloped its trunk entirely,
Then they can last together,
But if someone tries to separate them
Then the hazel tree dies quickly   75
And the honeysuckle at the same time.
"Beautiful love, so it is with us:
Neither you without me, nor I without you."
The Queen came riding along.
She looked along the slope of the path   80
And saw the stick of wood, she noticed it well,
And recognized all the letters on it.
The knights who escorted her
And who rode together with her
She ordered to stop: 85
She wanted to dismount and rest.
They obeyed her command.
She went far from her company
And called her maid,
Branguen, who was very faithful.   90
She went a little distance from the path
And in the woods she found him
Whom she loved more than any living being.
Together they had great joy.
He told her all he wanted   95
And she spoke to him of her pleasure.
Then she explained to him
How he would be reconciled with the King,
For it had much weighed on him
That he had banished Tristan;   100
He had done it because of an accusation.
Then she went away, she left her love,
But when it came to that separation
They began to weep.
Tristan returned to Wales   105
Until his uncle sent for him.
Because of the joy he had received
From his love, when he saw her,
And for the sake of what he had written to her [previously]
In order to remember the words,   110
As the Queen had told him to do,
Tristan, who played the harp well,
Composed a new *lai* about it.

I'll name it briefly:
The English call it "Goat's Leaf,"   115
The French "Chievrefoil."
I have spoken to you the truth
About the *lai* I have told here.

The hazel-honeysuckle metaphor is chosen by Marie de France in this *lai* to act as a distillate of the Tristan and Isolde legend's most powerful meanings, and to effect a final abolishment of separation, for, just like Tristan and Isolde, the violently separated tree and vine join in death.[9] The metaphor embodies the glorious and fatal paradox that, while attachment signifies life, and separation signifies death, when life is enforced separation, death may become transcendent union. In love, death must be more desirable than life, so the Tristan and Isolde myth tells us, because death, like erotic activity, "by dissolving the separate beings that participate in it, reveals their fundamental continuity, like the waves of a stormy sea" (Bataille 1962, 22). Death may provide a union that escapes the painful discontinuity and fragmentation of life. The metaphor also conveys the understanding, central to the love story, that all these elements— attachment, separation, union in death—are unavoidable. Both the fated beginning and the fatal ending are implied in the formulation of the metaphor and its explication by Tristan: "Neither you without me, nor I without you" (line 78). The remarkable economy of Marie de France's expression leaves no area of ambiguity concerning the implacable terms of the mythic events of union, dis-union, and re-union in death. This short episode of the famous story, as imagined and told by Marie, appears thus as an evocative and essentially complete shorthand version of the total legend.

The myth of Tristan and Isolde may also be seen as the myth of the encounter between civilization and wildness, an aspect included in "Chievrefoil" and, as we have seen, of particular importance to its author. In the legend and in the *lai*, as in many medieval literary works, the walls between civilization and non-civilization (the latter embodied by wild men and places) are not hermetically sealed, and one may go back and forth from one realm to the other. Civilization (in character, behaviour, appearance, speech) and non-civilization lie close together, both literally and figuratively. The myth of Tristan and Isolde is the myth of that difficult closeness, represented in the paradigmatically juxtaposed settings of the castle (site of the court and courtliness, of duties and constraints) and of the great forest of Morois (site of wildness and passion, of illegality and freedom). Their fall from moral and social grace excludes Tristan and Isolde from civilization, forcing them to seek shelter in the woods, like wild creatures, dressed in rags but free to pursue their "wild" passion. The Tristan and Isolde legend mythifies these social and moral dualisms: desire/punishment, freedom/banishment, private/public, wildness/civilization, woods/castle. After their fate has been determined by the drinking of the philter (on the sea, another "wild" space), the lovers are either hunted by others or drawn by their desire into the forest, which becomes a counter-castle, offering an alternative subversive security. But Tristan and Isolde are also drawn to the castle, where they feel they ought to be, fulfilling their traditional duties of liegeman and queen, surrounded by the society that *ought* to be theirs. The secondary myth of the problematic meeting between the wild demands of human desires and the strong call for an orderly integration into a group of one's peers is thus firmly embedded in the love story.

In Marie de France's "Chievrefoil," this secondary myth is again perfectly present in an encapsulated form. Tristan is clearly portrayed as the equivalent of a "wild man": exiled, he is prey to self-destructive despair (lines 19–20); when he returns surreptitiously to Cornwall in order to see Isolde he seeks out the solitary forest, and when he meets with the queen it is in the woods. The contrast is great between that twilight world and the world of the court, yet the two are intimately juxtaposed: the courtly entourage has to travel through the woods to arrive at Tintagel, where Mark is to hold his Pentecost court. Marie de France seems to convey a certain ambiguity in her perception of the distance between the court and the woods: when Isolde leaves the path where she is traveling with her barons and ladies in order to meet Tristan "she went far from her company" (line 88), but, at the same time, when she is about to reach him, "she went a little distance from the path" (line 91). Both close together and far apart, the two *loci* share a common goal: joy and pleasure, but in guises as radically opposed as the "joy and pleasure" (line 42) of the court and the "joy . . . pleasure" (lines 94, 96) of the lawless lovers. At the end of "Chievrefoil," a reconciliation between the two *loci* seems to take place when Tristan becomes in fact a *trouvère* and composes a new *lai*. His "courtly" gifts allow him to transcend and eternalize his "wild" experience. Unmitigated wildness begins and ends in the woods; in a context of civilization, it may become productive and creative.

The honeysuckle-hazel metaphor takes in the secondary myth the same meaning of inseparability and transcendence we have seen before, suggesting the necessary entwining of wildness and civilization, and offering a model to transcend the tension between the two through the creative act. Thus Marie de France formulates not only the persistent conflict between eros and civilization, but also a possible valorization of that conflict in terms of creative possibility.

While the primary myth (the joining of life and death) and its derivative (the conjunction of wildness and civilization) are clearly present in all the versions of the Tristan and Isolde tale, a tertiary myth may be seen in "Chievrefoil," a myth of the origin of literature, closely tied to the other two and deeply connected with Marie's interest in reconciling tradition and her own myth of Celtic orality. In this *lai*, she explores the relation, alternation, and interaction, between the two. In the customary introductory lines, she mentions an oral source, adding immediately, "And I have composed it in writing" (line 6), thus introducing the link between the two forms of expression on which she will build variations during the *lai*. When she enters into the narration, she structures the plot (the meeting between Tristan and Isolde) around the conveying of a message, resulting in a "brief encounter" between the lovers and a renewed separation.

The motif of the message is handled in a way that has caused a long controversy between scholars (Gagnon 1970; Freeman 1984). It is not immediately clear whether there are two messages—a preparatory one in writing, sent by Tristan to the queen prior to her arrival in the forest, and a later one, consisting of Tristan's name carved on a branch of hazel—or a single message carved on the stick, either spelling out the rather long (lines 63–78) description of Tristan and Isolde's love, maybe in runic script, or suggesting it by the mere evocative mention of Tristan's name. The former hypothesis of the two messages seems much more in keeping with the text; Marie de France clearly states that Tristan had sent a written letter to Isolde (lines 61–62). In this letter he would have spoken to her about their love and fate, using the famous metaphor, and he would also have alerted her to watch for the second message, namely the stick of hazel—a link with the metaphor—with his name on it, which would indicate to her where to find him.

If we accept this hypothesis (and there are in the above-mentioned controversy no convincing arguments against it), we see again an example of interaction between two forms of expression: an elaborate written one (the letter), and a more primitive one (the carving on the stick). Tristan is not "primitive," since he is capable of composing a written message, but he uses the primitive expression to activate, as it were, the civilized one. Thanks to the carved message on the stick, the written message of love and desire becomes, literally, alive, and gains concrete meaning in the actuality of the lovers' tryst in the forest. From the joining of the two messages, the two codes, pleasure and joy may result. This joy in turn produces a work of poetry (lines 107–13). We have then a sequence of writing/carving/writing, of "civilized" expression activated by "wild" expression, resulting in the yet higher (because endowed with the potential for permanence) "civilized" expression of the literary work. Tristan, the mythical reconciliator-author, a model for Marie, is seen as both encoder and decoder of the essential message, with the hazel-honeysuckle metaphor as the code for love, and, in abbreviated form (the hazel branch), for the concrete experience of love. The *lai* he composes is a perfect hermeneutic structure, encompassing the concept of passionate love and its enactment, the code and its explication. The "energizing" of the written message by the carved one suggests that the viable literary work is inseparable from its wild inspiration, and that only the conjunction of civilization and wildness, of tradition and difference, can produce a living poetry.

In *Myth and Language*, Albert Cook calls metaphor "literature's access to myth" and demonstrates how the metaphors in a literary work may liberate the rather closed dialectic of myth (such as we can see it, for instance, in a tribal culture or in any firmly established mythology), thus "enabling its components to enter into various relationships" (1980, chapter 10). Through the hazel-honeysuckle metaphor, Marie de France is able to link three mythic constructs: the erotic, the moral/social, and the aesthetic (which is also a deeply personal one). In all three constructs, joy plays the role of reward and justification: the erotic joy of Tristan and Isolde, the joy of the court (i.e., of civilization), and, finally, the joy of poetic activity. Several times in the *Lais*, Marie de France insists on the facts of creative pleasure, her own and that of the reader, and of desire, that is, her author's desire to draw on her "wild" material.

As a myth about the birth of writing—her writing—"Chievre-foil" reiterates Marie de France's intention to establish a unified origin for her literary project, an origin that will allow her to wed imagination to discipline, and to create meaningful links between her "good material" (as she dubs her Breton inspiration in line 1 of "Guigemar")—that is, the fruits of her selection or invention; her "poetic work" (Prolog, line 41), that is, her literary gift and vocation; and the limitless future of "memory" (Prolog, line 35) and of "fame" (Prolog, line 31), that is, her artistic reputation and survival. The myth expresses also Marie de France's concept of the author as lover and shaper of the material, and of the text as a product of that love and that impatient desire to give form.

Marie uses the primary myth of the fatal but exalting love, beset by obstacles and ending in death, and shifts its meaning to an exaltation of victorious creativity, ending in immortality. Her myth of the birth of writing is, no doubt, a very personal one in the sense that it solves for Marie several problems concerning the choice and treatment of fictional material, the role of the author, and the ultimate importance of the literary text. Her tertiary usage of the Tristan and Isolde legend allows her to steep the act of writing in the tensions of the primary myth and of its secondary meaning, and to resolve these tensions through the masterful invention of the hazel-honeysuckle metaphor, while retaining for the creative act the aura of passion and pleasure that marks the legend of Tristan and Isolde.

If in the Prolog Marie narrates the stages of her authorial development and progressive self-definition, in "Chievrefoil" she dramatizes her conception of the kind of author she is and must be. Tristan enacts the dangers, fears, and resolutions through which Marie passes in search of her authorial self. Tristan's exile from Isolde is thus a *mise en scène* of Marie's fear of exile from the realm of the Book.

As Tristan's banishment, deserved because of the illegitimacy of his love, is yet seen as unjust because of the brilliant supremacy of his desire, so Marie's banishment from writing, "normal" in conventional terms, is undeserved because of the superiority of her intellectual and artistic gifts, which should be allowed to triumph over convention: hence her first justification for writing in the Prolog.

As Tristan's exile plunges him into despair, and even brings him to the brink of self-destruction, so Marie has felt the intimations of despair, of the debilitating and undermining *acedia* that would become her stark reality were she to be separated from the Book: her second justification. As Tristan, the asocial, excluded one, uses wildness—the woods as hiding and trysting place, the stick as message—in pursuit of the object of his desire, so Marie uses the wildness of Celtic orality in pursuit of her desire: access to writing on her terms.

Tristan's composition, first of his letter to Isolde and of the carved message which prolongs it, and then of his *lai*, signifies the same combination and reconciliation of the sanctioned and the outlawed, the traditional and the unconventional, that we see performed by Marie in the Prolog. In both pieces remembrance is goal and result: the inscribing of the wild inspiration into the accepted artistic form guarantees survival into posterity. In both works Marie paints the portrait of the lover/author as an encoder in search of a decoder. As meaning is encoded into the hazel branch by Tristan to be read by Isolde, so the "ancient writers" of the Prolog encode an obscure meaning in their books, to be found, explicated, and thus completed by later readers who, in turn, may take their example, as Marie does, and encode meanings in their work for interpreters to decode. Into this chain of literature and literary tradition as a process of encoding and decoding, Marie de France introduces her own contribution: the myth of her Celticity/orality, seemingly obscure, accidental, or even frivolous, to be decoded eventually as the sign of her uniqueness and difference—that which allows her to write. Thus she is able to travel from the world of the Book, embodied in the Prolog in the figure of Priscian (well chosen, since he is not only a writer but a teacher and demonstrator of writing), to her own mythic, wild world of the pre-Book, in search of *her* unique Book, the ultimate object of her creative desire.

Notes

1. For information concerning the texts attributed to Marie de France, their dates as well as the possible identity of the writer, see Mickel (1974, 13–23). Mickel suggests, and it is an attractive suggestion, that Marie may also be the author of a

translation entitled "La vie Sainte Andree." Concerning the composition of the three works usually attributed to Marie, he proposes these dates: *Fables* and *Lais*, second half of the twelfth century; *Purgatory*, early thirteenth century.

Do the *Fables* antedate the *Lais*? I believe they do, on the following grounds:

a. The short prologue to the *Fables* contains, in embryonic form, some of the ideas Marie develops more articulately and extensively in the prologue to the *Lais*.

b. As Hanning and Ferrante point out, the *Lais* "make many of the same points [as the *Fables*] but in a far more subtle way" (1978, 9), so that they may be seen as the work of an author who has honed her craft.

c. The *Lais* certainly constitute the more daring work of the two, for here Marie creates her own source. It is likely that she tried her hand at a more conventional literary undertaking before embarking on a more original and audacious one.

d. In the opening lines of "Guigemar," Marie refers clearly to criticism she has undergone because of a previous work; in all likelihood this is the *Fables*.

2. Translated by Mickel (1974, 15). Denis Piramus's pointed remark concerning the truth of the *Lais* is clearly an answer to Marie's insistence throughout the work that what she writes is true; his remark serves as an example of critical confusion between psychological and factual truth. It is also a confirmation that he is talking about the Marie who signed her name to the pertinent group of twelve *lais*.

3. Some scholars would cast doubts on the identification of Marie's gender; see Huchet (1981). Peter Dronke comments on the tendency, especially in earlier scholarship, to attribute, *in toto* or in part, writings by medieval women—such as Hrotsvitha, Hildegard of Bingen, Heloise—to male authors (1984, ix).

4. For a treatment of the narrative *lai*, see Mickel (1974), who gives a useful synopsis of the critical debate concerning the term *lai* and the origins and nature of the genre. See also Freeman (1984), Baum (1968), and Rothschild (1974).

5. All quotes from the *Lais* are translated by me from Jean Rychner's edition.

6. See Burgess (1977), and also Rychner's bibliography and notes (1969).

7. The two concepts are inseparable for Marie. However, in the prologue to "Guigemar," after her more general remarks, she says in introducing this particular story that "according to the letter and the writing I shall tell you an adventure" (lines 23–24), which some critics have taken as a reference to a written source. Rychner, in the notes to his edition, quotes Gaston Paris' translation of the lines as "I'll show you in writing" and reminds the reader that the reference to a written source is a traditional *topos*, used as a guarantee of authenticity, the equivalent of the expression "literally." Paris' translation and interpretation do not do violence to the Old French text, and agree with Marie's insistence on *her* work, *her* writing.

8. Marie de France knew Ovid's "Philomela" (*Metamorphoses* vi). See Cargo (1966).

9. The following remarks on "Chievrefoil" have been taken in part from Sankovitch, "Tristan and Isolde: the Birth of Writing," presented at the First International Tristan and Isolde Conference, Boston 1985, and forthcoming in *Tristania*.

Marie de France: Works Cited

Fables. 1925. Ed. A. Ewert and R. C. Johnston. Oxford: Blackwell.
Lais. 1969. Ed. Jean Rychner. Paris: Champion.
L'Espurgatoire Seint Patriz. 1903. Ed. T. A. Jenkins. Chicago: University of Chicago Press.

For a complete list of manuscripts and editions, see Burgess (1977, 15-27).

Works Cited

Ardener, Edwin. 1975. "Belief and the Problem of Women." In *Perceiving Women.* Ed. Shirley Ardener, 1-27. London: Malaby Press.
Bataille, Georges. 1962. *Death and Sensuality. A Study of Eroticism and the Taboo.* New York: Walker and Company.
Baum, Richard. 1968. *Recherches sur les œuvres attribuées à Marie de France.* Heidelberg: Carl Winter.
Bloomfield, Morton. (1952) 1967. *The Seven Deadly Sins.* East Lansing: Michigan State University Press.
Bullock-Davies, Constance. 1981. "Marie de France: A Reassessment of the Narrative Technique in the *Lais.*" In *Court and Poet.* Sel. proc. of the Third Congress of the International Courtly Literature Society, 93-99. Liverpool: Francis Cairns.
Burgess, Glyn S. 1977. *Marie de France. An Analytical Bibliography.* London: Grant and Cutler.
Cargo, Robert T. 1966. "Marie de France's "Le Laüstic" and Ovid's *Metamorphoses.*" *Comparative Literature* 18: 162-66.
Clifford, Paula. 1982. *Marie de France: Lais.* London: Grant and Cutler.

Cook, Albert. 1980. *Myth and Language*. Bloomington: Indiana University Press.

Curtius, E. R. (1948) 1963. *European Literature and the Latin Middle Ages*. Trans. Willard R. Trask. New York: Harper and Row.

Daly, Mary. 1978. *Gyn/Ecology: The Metaethics of Radical Feminism*. Boston: Beacon Press.

Delumeau, Jean. 1983. *Le Péché et la Peur*. Paris: Fayard.

Dragonetti, Roger. 1980. *La vie de la lettre au Moyen Age*. Paris: Editions du Seuil.

Dronke, Peter. 1984. *Women Writers of the Middle Ages*. Cambridge: Cambridge University Press.

Ferrante, Joan. 1975. *Woman as Image in Medieval Literature: From the Twelfth Century to Dante*. New York: Columbia University Press.

———. 1980. "The Education of Women in the Middle Ages in Theory, Fact, and Fantasy." In *Beyond Their Sex: Learned Women of the European Past*. Ed. Patricia Labalme, 9–42. New York: New York University Press.

———. "The French Courtly Poet: Marie de France." In *Medieval Women Writers*. Ed. K. M. Wilson, 64–89. Athens: University of Georgia Press.

Flahault, Patrick. 1972. *L'Extrême existence: Essai sur des représentations mythiques de l'intériorité*. Paris: François Maspéro.

Foulet, Alfred, and K. D. Uitti. 1981. "The Prologue to the *Lais* of Marie de France: A Reconsideration." *Romance Philology* 35: 242–49.

Fowles, John. 1974. *The Ebony Tower*. Boston: Little, Brown.

———. 1978. Foreword, *The Lais of Marie de France*. Trans. Robert Hanning and Joan Ferrante. New York: Dutton.

Freeman, Michelle. 1984. "Marie de France's Poetics of Silence: The Implications for a Feminine *Translatio*." *PMLA* 99: 860–83.

Gagnon, Maurice. 1970. "*Chievrefoil* and the Ogamic Tradition." *Romania* 91: 238–55.

Gold, Penny Schine. 1985. *The Lady and the Virgin: Image, Attitude and Experience in Twelfth-Century France*. Chicago: University of Chicago Press.

Hanning, Robert, and Joan Ferrante, trans. 1978. *The Lais of Marie de France*. New York: Dutton.

Herm, Gerhard. 1975. *The Celts*. London: Weidenfeld and Nicholson.

Hoepffner, Ernest. 1939. *Les Lais de Marie de France*. Paris: Nizet.

Huchet, Jean-Charles. 1981. "Nom de femme et écriture féminine au Moyen Age: Les *Lais de Marie de France*." *Poétique* 48: 407–30.

Husband, Timothy. 1980. *The Wild Man: Medieval Myth and Symbolism*. New York: Metropolitan Museum of Art.

Knapton, Antoinette. 1975. *Mythe et Psychologie chez Marie de France.* North Carolina Studies in the Romance languages and Literatures, 142. Chapel Hill: University of North Carolina Press.

Lawson, Lise. 1981. "La Structure du récit dans les *Lais* de Marie de France." In *Court and Poet.* Sel. proc. of the Third Congress of the International Courtly Literature Society, 233–40. Liverpool: Francis Cairns.

Le Goff, Jacques. 1964. *La Civilisation de l'Occident Médiéval.* Paris: Arthaud.

Lenaghan, R. T., ed., 1967. *Caxton's Aesop.* Cambridge: Harvard University Press.

Lipking, Lawrence. 1981. *The Life of the Poet.* Chicago: University of Chicago Press.

Malvern, Marjorie M. 1983. "Marie de France's Ingenious Uses of the Authorial Voice and Her Singular Contribution to Western Literature." *Tulsa Studies in Women's Literature* 2: 21–41.

Markale, Jean. 1976. *Les Celtes et la Civilisation Celtique.* Paris: Payot.

Ménard, Phillipe. 1979. *Les Lais de Marie de France: contes d'amour et d'aventure du Moyen Age.* Paris: Presses Universitaires de France.

Mickel, Emanual J., Jr. 1974. *Marie de France.* New York: Twayne.

Muir, Lynette R. 1985. *Literature and Society in Medieval France: The Mirror and the Image 1100–1500.* New York: St. Martin's Press.

Rothschild, Judith Rice. 1974. *Narrative Technique in the Lais of Marie de France.* North Carolina Studies in the Romance Languages and Literatures, 139. Chapel Hill: University of North Carolina Press.

de Rougemont, Denis. 1939. *L'Amour et l'Occident.* Paris: Plon.

Rychner, Jean, ed. 1969. *Les Lais de Marie de France.* Paris: Honoré Champion.

Showalter, Elaine. 1985. "Feminist Criticism in the Wilderness." In *The New Feminist Criticism.* Ed. E. Showalter, 243–70. New York: Pantheon Books.

Sienaert, Edgar. 1978. *Les Lais de Marie de France: du conte merveilleux à la nouvelle psychologique.* Paris: Champion.

Zumthor, Paul. 1972. *Essai de poétique médiévale.* Paris: Editions du Seuil.

Marguerite of Navarre presents a book to the Duchess of Etampes. Sixteenth
century miniature. From the Bibliothèque du Musée Condé, Chantilly. Reprinted by permission of GIRAUDON/ Art Resource, New York, New York.

≫ 2 ≪

The Dames des Roches

The Female Muse

> Women often describe the emergence of their talent as an infusion from a male master rather than inspiration from sexual commerce with a female muse.
>
> Susan Gubar

Where we know very little about the identity and the life of Marie de France, we are quite well informed concerning Madeleine (ca. 1520–87) and Catherine (1542–87) des Roches.[1] A mother and daughter from Poitiers, they wrote and published together a substantial body of work, consisting of poems, prose dialogues of a philosophical and pedagogical nature, translations of Latin texts, letters, and even a tragicomedy on a biblical subject, namely the story of Sarah and Tobias.

Widely known and highly admired in their time and circle, they have been more or less forgotten by later generations of readers and scholars. When they are mentioned in histories of literature, it is usually because of their early role in the creation of the *salon* and of the *genre épistolaire*. Scholars agree that their correspondence was the first by women to be published in French, and that the circle of learned and cultivated people they attracted to their Poitiers drawing room for serious conversation as well as for occasional, more frivolous, *jeux de société*, constituted indeed a full-fledged *salon*, one of the predecessors of the famous gatherings of the seventeenth century

(Diller 1936; McFarlane 1974; Keating 1941). One of those "society games" has also contributed to their survival in literary lore: during a particularly brilliant gathering at their *salon* on the occasion of the *Grands Jours*—or Great Assizes, a prestigious juridic assembly—held in Poitiers from 10 September to 18 December 1579, a flea was seen on the bosom of Catherine des Roches; it promptly inspired a spate of poetic variations in Greek, Latin, and French by many famous humanists, scholars, and lawyers, all would-be or accredited poets. Their contributions on the theme of that happy flea were gathered in a volume appropriately called *La Puce de Madame des Roches*. In the last decade or so, the Dames have been anthologized, especially in collections of early feminist writings by women, and sporadic but deserved attention has been paid to particular aspects of their work, such as Catherine's narrative powers (Pérouse 1977, 218–26), and the Dames' interest in learning (Larsen, 1987).

Madeleine and Catherine des Roches were well educated, and for their contemporaries their erudition was the salient fact about them. Many of their visitors and familiars—among whom we count such eminent personalities, humanists, lawyers, poets, and literary scholars as Joseph-Justus Scaliger, Etienne Pasquier, Claude Pellejay, Claude Binet, Charles Tiraqueau, Agrippa d'Aubigné, Jacques Pelletiers du Mans, and the brothers Sainte-Marthe, to name only a few— bear witness to their extraordinary learning: extraordinary, that is, for women, for in that age of scholarship and humanistic study, learned men abounded all over Europe.

Joseph-Justus Scaliger, who had come to live in the province of Poitou in 1574 and who became a good friend and a great admirer of the Dames, describes Madeleine as "the most learned person in Europe, although she knows only one language."[2] It is clear that by "person" he means here "woman" (as in the French phrase "une personne du sexe," i.e., a woman). As for the "one language," it must be Latin, since Madeleine's native French would not be counted as a language acquired by special knowledge. Catherine also knew Latin, as well as Italian and probably Greek. In several of his letters, Etienne Pasquier has testified eloquently as to the impression made by the Dames' interest in intellectual matters. To his friend Pithou, a Parisian lawyer, he describes in a lively fashion the ambiance of the women's house: "I assure you that their house is a true school of honor. In the morning you'll find the mother and the daughter, after having

taken care of household matters, sitting over their books, now composing a learned poem, now a well-written letter. During the hours
after dinner and after supper [i.e., afternoons and evenings] their
door is open to all men of culture. There is talk then on all sorts of
subjects, now on philosophy, now on history, or about the events of
our time, or about some other interesting topic. Nobody who enters
there leaves without being more intelligent or having learned something" (Pasquier [1723] 1976, 2, bk. 6:8). Pasquier also has called
them, in an earlier letter, "the honor of the city of Poitiers, and of our
century" (2, bk. 6:7) while the contemporary biographer La Croix du
Maine dubs them "the two pearls of all Poitou."

In his *Bibliothèques Françaises* La Croix du Maine remarks that
"these two ladies are so learned, and have such a vast knowledge of
all good literature that (on top of the published testimony to that
effect by the most erudite minds of France) their own writings are
that learning's most true and faithful expression, and as much the
writings they have published as those which are as yet unpublished."
He also notes that "they are still alive today and flourishing in
Poitiers this very year [1584]; and they do not stop working, in order
to make themselves immortal and worthy of perpetual glory" (La
Croix du Maine [1584, 1585] 1969).

The preoccupation with the world of the Book, that is, for them,
with learning as a path to poetry and hence to immortality, is central
to the work and thought of the Dames. A second, related key-notion
in their life as well as in their work is their closeness to each other. It
is therefore necessary to explore these two themes—desire for
learning/Poetry/immortality and the exceptionally strong bonds between the two Dames—in order to understand fully the myth Catherine created to express and justify their yearning toward the life of
study and creativity, toward the world of the Book.

Living as they did in a period of great intellectual and poetic
ferment, when the most celebrated French poets, such as the members of the noted Pléiade group,[3] were also humanists (i.e., dedicated, serious, students of the language, literature, and history of
Latin and Greek antiquity, as well as the works of the Italian lin-
guists, poets, and philosophers who had been their predecessors in
the humanistic enterprise), the Dames had to embrace the concept of
learning and poetry as one and indivisible. In the circle they created
for and around themselves in Poitiers, that concept would have been

taken for granted. The Pléiade poets also stressed the need for divine inspiration, for "poetic fury," but it was essential to acquire the necessary linguistic and intellectual skills in order to gain entry into "the mythic Platonic chain of the transmission of poetic fury" (Demerson 1972, 552). At the beginning of this chain, where we find the truly divinely inspired mythological or half-mythic figures such as Orpheus or Homer, the poets were "naturally" endowed with the highest poetic gifts, and had no need of artificially acquired learning. But this original perfection did not survive intact; sixteenth century poets "were necessarily 'human' poets, that is to say they could no longer rely exclusively upon inspiration from the divinity" (Castor 1964, 41). In order to establish and maintain contact with the world of their divine predecessors, study and scholarship were essential for the Renaissance poets, allowing them to penetrate into the world of the greatest Greek and Roman poets, and into that of the later authors, followers, and imitators of the truly divine ones: those who kept that poetry and that culture alive. Ignorance is the enemy of poetry, as the Pléiade poets assert repeatedly, and, in the words of Ronsard, "the Muses are in study and in knowledge" (1950, "La Lyre"). Without study and knowledge, the Pléiade theory of creative imitation (or, as du Bellay ([1549] 1972) sees it, "innutrition" by contact with the nourishing predecessor-texts), as well as the pervasive presence in Pléiade poetry of Greek and Roman mythology, would be unthinkable. The Dames des Roches were familiar with all these ideas, both through their readings and through the discussions that must have taken place in their *salon,* and they possessed, as we have seen, quite a remarkable education and knowledge themselves.

The debate about a liberal education for women was a lively one in the Renaissance, and a consensus seems never to have been achieved on the subject (Kelso 1956; Bainton 1980). Between those who were of the opinion that education would be useless for women, whose sex destined them for marriage and maternity exclusively, and those who would give girls much the same instruction as boys, including a sound knowledge of Latin and Greek as a basis, all shadings of opinion are represented in the many writings dedicated to the controversy, in which the Dames des Roches themselves participated, as we shall see. Their reality was that of the upper middle class of Poitiers, and in that milieu they were the exceptions rather than the rule. The sometimes exaggerated praise of their male acquaintances makes it clear that they fall out of the ordinary run of women of their class, as do the following words from Madeleine to her female contemporaries in an "Epistre aux Dames" (Letter to the ladies), which prefaces the *Œuvres:*

> It is my opinion that the word, true image of the soul, and the fugitive voice fixed on the paper, give a certain indication, not only of the richness of the mind and of its acquired or natural gifts, but of the authentic integrity of those who speak or write. That is why I want, ladies, in this little work in which I have painted myself, to take the time to assure you of the friendship I have always felt for you. . . . If you advise me that silence, ornament of women, may cover mistakes of language and of understanding, I will answer you that silence may indeed prevent shame, but cannot increase honor, and that speaking separates us from the witless beasts.[4]

Madeleine does not take approval by eventual women readers for granted, and feels that a strong justification for writing is needed in an age and in a milieu in which women were more likely to be praised for their *taciturnitas* than for their literary prowess. In the "Epistre à sa Mere" (Letter to her mother) in the same volume, Catherine also offers a "spirited and ironic defense not only of her own work and person, but of all women who sought to write and publish" (Larsen 1984, 59) noting that "whereas there are more than enough men who write, there are few women who involve themselves in such a practice."[5] There were well-educated women who were interested in literature and sometimes engaged in writing (Feugère [1860] 1969), but they were a small minority.

It is not clear how Madeleine acquired her learning, but we may speculate that as a young woman she must have been stimulated and encouraged by the current of intellectual renewal and enthusiasm for poetry which made Poitiers from ca. 1545 to ca. 1555 a center of cultural life and initiative. Later it is the mother who takes care of the daughter's education and instruction, as their contemporaries have confirmed. Madeleine was married twice. First, in 1539, she married André Fradonnet, with whom she had a son, Nicolles, and two daughters, Catherine and Lucrèce. Nicolles and Lucrèce did not survive babyhood, and Fradonnet died in 1547. In 1550, Madeleine married the highly esteemed lawyer, François Eboissard (+ 1578) with whom she did not have children. Catherine was thus an only daughter, and Madeleine was free to concentrate all her pedagogical fervor on her, maybe supplementing the instruction she was able to provide herself by hiring tutors who would teach Catherine in such areas as Greek language and literature.

In spite of their own solid education, however, the Dames were very aware of the problems access to learning—to the Book—usually posed for women. Speaking, no doubt, for women in general, Madeleine laments that "our parents have the laudable custom,/ In order to deprive us of the use of our wits,/ Of keeping us locked up at home/ And of handing us the spindle instead of the pen" (*Œuvres*, Ode 1). Although her own second marriage seems to have been a happy one, marriage *per se* was not seen by Madeleine as conducive to the pleasure of free intellectual and artistic pursuits: "We are promised freedom and pleasure,/ And then we pay with persistent suffering/ When we bring our dowry under the laws of marriage," she says in the same poem. The "dowry" she speaks of is not so much the financial contribution to the new household each bride was expected to bring with her as the stock of intellectual and creative gifts that, once entered "under the laws of marriage" a woman was no longer free to enjoy and explore as she pleased. Still in the same poem, Madeleine denounces these "laws" with vigour, says she would like "to show men/ How much their laws commit violence upon us," and elsewhere she complains that "men have all the authority,/ Against reason and against equity" (*Œuvres*, "Epistre à ma Fille").

What "laws" does Madeleine have in mind? The legal status of women in the sixteenth century was extremely complex, and there are, as Ian Maclean points out, "various models of equalization of the sexes . . . which reflect differing priorities and different degrees of conservatism" (1984, chapter 5). A group of documents cited by George Diller prove that Madeleine and Catherine des Roches were able and free to manage their own financial and legal matters—sales and leases of real estate, loans, lawsuits and foreclosures against delinquent debtors—efficiently and independently. Nevertheless, it is true that on the whole restrictions existed on the legal rights of women and that "in spite of regional and national differences, the principle of woman's inferiority [was] almost universal" (Maclean 1980, 81). But I believe that Madeleine, speaking out against male laws in the context of the desirability of learning, attacks less a *de jure* than a *de facto* social situation which, by limiting women's choices of occupation and by enacting an almost exclusive preference for marriage, in effect curtails women's primary or continued access to the education that would open the doors to creativity. While girls could, if they wished and if their parents permitted it, engage in learning and in writing, the promise of liberty and pleasure implicit in these pursuits was an unreliable one, since marriage, the natural destiny of women, "inseparable from the notion of woman" (Maclean 1980, 75), with its duties and responsibilities, would soon put an end to the unhampered intercourse with books and pen:

> The most beautiful days of our green years
> Resemble the flowers of a gracious Spring,
> Threatened by tempest, by wind and rain,
> Which will put a stop to our flight.
>
> In the happy time of my past season,
> My wings were well fastened to my side,
> But, in losing my young freedom
> Before I could fly, my feather [my pen] was broken.
>
> I should like to sit over my books,
> And, sighing, confide my sorrows to the paper,
> But some occupation always comes up to pull me away,
> Reminding me that I must follow my profession.

In these stanzas (*Œuvres*, Ode 1) Madeleine switches from the first person plural to the first person singular, indicative of her own bitter experience. Marriage as a "profession" does not encourage the free pursuit of learning as the professions of the Dames' male acquaintances and intellectual equals do: philosophers, teachers, lawyers, poets, they may continue in the path for which their liberal education had prepared them: "Freedom, expansion of powers, recreation, and delight are the lures to tempt boys to arduous effort in mastery of the world's best minds" (Kelso 1956, 58). For young women, these lures prove treacherous as education's pleasures vanish before the demands of that other dominant model, that of the *mulier economica*, the domestic woman/wife/mother.

The example of the Italian women humanists is not encouraging in this respect. The situation has been summed up by King and Rabil in the following way: "In every case the women, as young girls, were

encouraged and strongly supported in their studies. They were recognized by their families, by male humanists, and by their cities as
prodigies. Those women, however, who aspired to continue a humanist career into their adult years were not greeted with the encouragement and praise they had received as prodigies, but icily and with
hostility. . . . Two socially acceptable alternatives were open to
women. One was marriage, the other religious vows. Many chose
marriage, and of those who did only one maintained her humanist
studies intensely after marriage" (1983, 25–26).

The Dames des Roches were familiar with the life and work of
at least one of these learned Italian women, Cassandra Fedele (1465–
1558), praised for her learning by the Florentine poet and humanist
Angelo Poliziano in a glowing letter to which Catherine alludes
twice. Cassandra, who had been a youthful wonder, was married off
when she could no longer qualify as a prodigy because of her age.
After her marriage she suffered from chronic illness. When, after a
hiatus of seventeen years, she returned to literary work, she never
fulfilled her early promise (King and Rabil 1983, 21–23).

While marriage thus separates women from learning, Madeleine des Roches recognizes, in a sarcastic statement, that it is the
prevalent socially accepted and acceptable ideal for women: "A
woman who is smart enough/ To spin and keep house,/ That is really
more profitable" (Œuvres, Ode 3). Nevertheless, after evoking such
"accepted" female occupations as gossiping and dressing up, she
repeats, in the same poem, that "There is something more
worthy . . . that is to choose the ink and the pen/ And to use them
intelligently."

The pen-spindle opposition, a commonplace in the debate concerning woman's role, in which these objects function as emblems of
learning and creativity on the one hand and of domesticity on the
other, appears frequently in the Dames' writing. While the pen has
been seen by male authors as a metaphorical penis (Gilbert and Gubar 1979, 1), Madeleine des Roches' "plume" (pen and feather) is
associated with "ailes" (wings) and therefore with the freedom of the
unfettered flight of the imagination and the intellect. "I'd rather write
than spin" she declares, and opts for the productive enterprise of
study and literature, which she sees as "the art which, taking matter/
Can confirm upon it its most complete form" (Œuvres, Epistre à ma
Fille). She echoes Ronsard and the convictions of all the humanist
poets when, in the same "Epistre," she urges her daughter to fulfill
her duty "toward the Muses and divine knowledge."

Catherine's contribution to the debate concerning women's education consists mainly of two rather lengthy dialogues included in the *Secondes Œuvres*. The first is the conversation between Severe and Placide. Severe complains bitterly to his neighbor, Placide, about the difficulties of living with his wife, a contemptuous, rebellious, angry shrew, and his daughter, a frivolous, affected, flighty nincompoop. Placide, a widower, speaks glowingly about *his* daughter, Pasithee, who passes her time in the study of such authors as Plutarch and Senecca. When Severe expresses surprise that Placide allows the girl such liberty in view of "the imbecillities of these little beasties" (i.e., young girls) and of the well-known fact that learned women are monsters, Placide launches into a fervent defense of female education. To Severe's remark that "her [i.e., woman's] hand must touch the spindle and not the book," Placide replies that the two are not mutually exclusive, thus adopting a recurrent humanistic argument that learning will help girls to become better wives, mothers, and household managers. At the end of the conversation Severe promises that he will send his daughter, Iris, to visit Pasithee. The second dialogue then takes place between the two young women, with Pasithee extolling the pleasures and advantages of learning, and the empty-headed Iris expressing reservations, such as that learned ladies do not attract young gentlemen.

While there are no original contributions to the debate about women's education in these pieces, they formulate the usual arguments in a lively and amusing way. What is lacking in Catherine's neatly turned and entertaining little *tableaux* is the sense of indignation and urgency that mark Madeleine's opinions on the subject. Of course, Catherine had always been left free to pursue the intellectual life. Never married, always sheltered by her mother, she did not experience the hiatus, so painful in Madeleine's existence, between early promise ("my past season") and a much delayed fulfillment: Madeleine did not start to publish until 1578, when she was almost sixty years old. But this does not mean that Catherine was less committed to her mother's goal of creativity through study, and it does not mean that she ignored the problems inherent in her chosen career as woman writer. In the dialogue between Severe and Placide, she makes fun of Severe, a caricatural misogynist, who calls women like herself monsters. And although Placide rebukes him by saying that "monsters are not always signs of Nature's error, but they often show how great her power is," Catherine may have felt at times the "monstrous" anomaly of her position with less than enjoyment.

While she often shows pride in her own and her mother's difference from the norm, in the following sonnet from the *Œuvres* she demonstrates also an unmistakable and painful ambivalence:

To my Spindle

My spindle and my care, I promise you and swear,
To love you forever, and never to exchange
Your domestic honor for a good which is strange,
Which, inconstant, wanders, and tends its foolish snare.

With you at my side, dear, I feel much more secure
Than with paper and ink arrayed all around me
For, if I needed defending, there you would be
To rebuff any danger, to help me endure.

But, spindle, my dearest, I do not believe
That, much as I love you, I will come to grief
If I do not quite let that good practice dwindle
Of writing sometimes, if I give you fair share,
If I write of your merit, my friend and my care,
And hold in my hand both my pen and my spindle.

In this poem Catherine's hesitation between pen and spindle is expressed with a poignant awareness of the fragmentation and division of the female self which, torn between the call of creativity and the urgings of woman's "normal" role, hesitates and tries, tremulously and unsuccessfully, to effect a reconciliation, the coexistence rather flippantly suggested by Placide, which, in a woman's life, is so often doomed to fail.[6] In Pasquier's letter, we have seen how the Dames' domestic occupations, and especially their social function as hostesses, took up a great deal of their time, and while their *salon* afforded them certainly much interest and pleasure, the need to be always available to callers must also have felt at times an obstacle and a burden. If they wanted to participate in the learned exchanges necessary to their self-image and to their need for intellectual intercourse, the Dames had no way to do it but through their *salon*.

In the opening lines of her sonnet, Catherine addresses the spindle almost as if it were a husband, calling it her "care" (that is, the "normal" focus of her preoccupations and occupations), and abandoning her freedom to it in quasi-legalistic terms of promise and oath. Its "domestic honor" is opposed to "the good which is strange," which is presented, as it were, as the lover, and is the poetic act, the female muse, seductive and alien, promising pleasure as well as risk. In the second stanza Catherine names the alien good: paper and ink, but weakens it at the same time. The conventional spindle protects, while paper and ink leave a woman vulnerable and exposed to unspecified danger. Their presence is enveloping but ineffective. The tone changes in the third stanza, when Catherine now addresses the spindle as "m'amie," that is, as a woman, as weak. It is only through that subterfuge that she dares to suggest that she be allowed to indulge in creating poetry, which is now called "that good practice," in terms more suggestive of duty than of pleasure. The possibility of writing exists only through that spurious transformation, which confers on writing the legitimacy of the traditional occupation. Even so there are reservations: "sometimes." In the last two lines, the spindle occupies again the dominant place of the husband, as "care" adorned with "merit" now usurps the substance of any possible prospective writing, becoming its only permissible subject, and in effect eliminates the joys of free creativity the "alien good" might have brought. Torn between the pen and the spindle, between the female muse and the male-originated conventionality, both of which represent, torturingly, herself and not-herself, Catherine seems here mutilated and alienated, whether she opts for one or the other.

This poem, however significant, represents only an episode of discouragement in Catherine's work. In most of her writings, she is much more optimistic concerning women's possibilities. In a "Bergerie" included in the *Secondes Œuvres* we read:

> Let's sing freedom,
> For the freedom of women
> Is the most beautiful light
> Which could shine in their souls.

Like her mother, Catherine is less interested in freedom in the legal sense of the word than in the spiritual and ideological freedom that will allow women to develop their talents, cultivate their gifts, and explore the world—the enticing, promising world of the Book.

We may well ask: Why this burning desire and determination, in spite of all problems, doubts, difficulties? There are probably many interwoven and complex reasons, but one is stated repeatedly throughout the Dames' work: they want for themselves what male poets see as their ultimate reward: poetic immortality. The *topos* of immortality, bestowed by poets upon those whom they sing and upon themselves by the excellence of their singing may be traced to Homer, Pindar, and Plato (Clements 1942, chapter 2), and the Renaissance poets knew it best in its Horatian formulation of "exegi monumentum," (I have erected a monument). In French poetry of the sixteenth century, it is a commonplace, taken for granted and constantly referred to in the writings of the Pléiade. Paraphrases of the Horatian formula abound, as the poets assert over and over again their confidence in the immortality that poetic work guarantees.

The *topos* should not be confused with the *topos* of glory with which it is sometimes identified. Glory is a worldly, temporal, and therefore fragile thing, and it is thus not surprising that poets often treat it with contempt, and that anti-glory also becomes a poetic theme (Clements 1942, 51ff.). While the scepticism toward glory extends sometimes to the belief in poetic immortality, it is more likely to be based on a disenchantment with society (especially with the *vulgum plebs*, the vulgar and ignorant masses), and to be therefore limited to the rewards—material or spiritual—the poet may expect in this world.

As far as eternity goes, the concept of poetry as perpetuation is dominant. Poetry saves from death the singer and the sung. Women have generally belonged to the second category, and thus have depended for immortality on the whims of the poets who loved and admired them. But for the Dames des Roches this is far from enough. Women must conquer immortality for themselves by their own writing; they must erect their own monument. We have seen in Marie de France the same desire for survival in memory, survival through work. For most women, oblivion—disappearance into the death of total non-remembrance—is the expected lot.[7] Access to deeds and works that might guarantee immortality is limited and therefore all the more desirable. Madeleine des Roches tells women: "You can by yourselves/ Take revenge on pale death/ Without having to beg another writer" (*Œuvres*, Ode 3), and Catherine, in the same volume's "Epistre à sa Mere," blames women who "want to be seen by their most obliging suitors in the hope that the latter will celebrate worthily their beauty, even though they themselves have it within their power to sing themselves."[8]

For male authors, that power of self-expression, grounded in their legitimate descent from the divine father, Apollo, whom Ronsard calls "Father, Cynthian Phoebus/ Oh holy Apollo" (1950, Odes 1:20), and confirmed by the well-established and revered lineage of male poets and poetry, may be taken for granted. Ronsard sees himself and all other poets, ancient and contemporary, as the sons of a divine father, and he addresses them as "you honored singers,/ Who in this base world/ Owe your birth/ To golden-haired Apollo." For women poets that fabled paternity is meaningless, and a coherent genealogy is nonexistent. It is not to the father-son bond of Apollo and his descendants but to the mother-daughter tie that the Dames des Roches turn for the authority empowering them to write, since their own closeness is the primary source of their creative strength.

Their closeness was obviously a subject for discussion among their contemporaries. In his letter 8 to Pithou, Pasquier, after his warm praises of the Dames' house, its inmates, and its stimulating atmosphere, writes that "there is only one thing which displeases me in that house, namely that the daughter, perfectly beautiful in body and mind as she is, rich in property, since she is the only heir of her mother, has been asked for her hand in marriage by a great number of highly placed men, yet has refused all these proposals, determined to live and die with her mother."[9]

It is normal that Pasquier should be displeased since Catherine, by refusing marriage, foils the circulation of body and property that would constitute her "normal" function, and takes herself, so to speak, "out of circulation," the circulation that is the basis of society and a guarantee of its perpetuation. Catherine is delinquent in her duty in the eyes of Pasquier and, no doubt, most contemporaries, both as a woman and as a member of her class. For the Dames, however, their closeness, which Catherine's marriage would have inevitably interrupted, was the one sure guarantee of continued creativity, as their mother-daughter relationship of giving and receiving biological life is paralleled by a reciprocal life-giving creative exchange.

This is affirmed in each of the "Epistres" they address to each other at the beginning of their respective contributions to each of the volumes they publish together. In the Œuvres, Madeleine thanks her daughter for having given her, from childhood on, the love and support that have enabled her to resist discouragement and despair, while Catherine acknowledges the importance of her mother's example. In the *Secondes Œuvres*, Madeleine writes to her daughter: "Let us continue in that union which has always kept us strong, and let us pray the Divine power always to guide the work, the thought, and the words of the two of us." Catherine says to Madeleine:

> You have given me life as Prometheus did to the earthen image which he himself formed, and neither was the fire lacking, for that was given to you by Heaven.[10] Knowing that I receive from you not only this mortal life, but the life of my life, I follow you everywhere as the shadow follows the body, and just as neither the body in its shape nor the shadow in its projection may be seen without the grace of light, so the lively clarity of your wisdom lights us the way on the little-used path where, my mother, I hope we will gather more olive branches than holly.

In the *Missives*, Madeleine recognizes her debt to Catherine: "My daughter, you who by the flight of your pen, without begging for anybody's help, take the trouble to free me from the Cimmerian nights in which ignorance and old age kept me buried, you resemble the green twig which never forgets the old stump which has given it a little formless matter. . . . Your strength encourages me to speak in public [i.e., to publish]," and Catherine expresses her happiness in the continued physical and spiritual presence of her mother.

Mary Daly laments the "fundamental lost bonding . . . the bond between mothers and daughters" (1978, 346), and Adrienne Rich writes that "the cathexis between mother and daughter . . . is the great unwritten story" (1976, 225). In their language of giving birth and form, of setting free, of conferring upon each other the strength of speaking, the light of wisdom, the fire of creativity, Madeleine and Catherine write about their bonding, and describe the cathexis between them, as through each other they direct it toward the poetic enterprise, ultimate object of their joined desire. Gayatri Spivak has remarked that "the restoration of a continuous bond between mother and daughter even *after* the 'facts' of gestation, birthing, and suckling, is indeed of great importance as a persistent effort against the sexism of millenia" (1981, 183) but warns that that bond may well be co-opted by the dominant male structure. The Dames avoid that danger by making the bond between them not an end in itself, but the basis of their creative project.

For them, this bond seems to exclude the significant presence of men. While men are of course present in the Dames' lives— Madeleine's husbands,[11] Catherine's suitors, their numerous acquaintances, visitors, and friends—they remain marginal and, as we have seen, sometimes disapproving observers of the Dames' only real, essential intimacy, that with each other.

Catherine has written a great many love poems, but in reading them we agree with George Diller that they are no more than slick literary exercises on a fashionable theme, and, for the greatest part, not very original ones (1936, 124ff.). In her letters to men she adopts frequently a precious-flirtatious tone, but she is entirely matter-of-fact when rebuking an overly insistent suitor: "I thought that my silence, together with my mother's letter, would have been sufficient answer to your letter. But since you desire a message which would clearly mirror my thought, I want to present that thought as frankly as possible. You should know, sir, that I would not feel myself free enough if I caused servitude in another. Not desiring a servant, I ask neither for a master nor for a companion. It will be enough for me if virtue commands me, good fortune attends me, and learning and writing serve me" (*Missives* 44).

For Catherine, marriage is a servitude and must therefore be rejected in favor of its opposite, chastity. Chastity is for her less a matter of sexual than of intellectual and social status. To be chaste means to be free from love which, for her, seems to mean chiefly the threat of marriage with its attendant duties, burdens, and distractions. To be chaste means to be free to follow one's own inclinations and taste. For Catherine, love and learning cannot be compatible, since she translates them as freedom and servitude. In a conversation among Love, Beauty, and Physis or Nature, Beauty, harassed by Love, declares her intention to go to the temple of Pallas, "so that I may save myself from Love's tyranny by books" and she calls that refuge "my temple of freedom" (*Œuvres*). In a sonnet addressed by Charite to Sincero (respectively the *personae* of the female and male lovers in Catherine's writings) Charite declares that she does not want to subject Sincero to rigorous laws—as Catherine had declined a suitor's servitude in the above-quoted letter—and that "I'll be pleased with you if you choose/ The time most appropriate for serious work:/ Do not tell me your amorous plaints/ Except when you have nothing else to do./ For the most of your time, stay with your studies" (*Œuvres*).

Margaret King notes that "chastity was expressive of the learned woman's defiance of the established natural order, and of the learned man's attempt to constrain her energies by making her mind the prison of her body" (1980, 78). For Catherine, chastity is a defense against male intrusion not only of the body but of the mind, and it is therefore indispensable for the access to the Book and books. Her frequent praise of chastity contains, indeed, a note of defiance, as it expresses her admiration for female strength and freedom. In the two pieces she writes in the *Œuvres* about the Amazons—"Pour une Mascarade d'Amazones" and "Chanson des Amazones"—she exalts the aggressive power of these fearless women warriors who have reversed the established, the "natural" order: in their land men are the subjected creatures: "We keep the men/ In our countries/ All busily spinning:/ Their cowardly wits/ Do not deserve/ To take up more beautiful work." The Amazons owe their power to their chastity, and from their battles carry back myrtle and laurel, symbols of glory and immortality. A male poet, such as Ronsard, may reject the warlike attributes of the Amazons: "It is better that the glory/ Of women should live in memory/ Through more gentle and pleasing deeds/ Than through those of the Amazons" ("Ode à Madame Marguerite"). For Catherine, however, they represent the possibility of autonomy and glory. The most powerful of all is the Amazon queen "Otrera, daughter of Martesia." Catherine des Roches' source here is clearly Boccaccio's *De Claris Mulieribus* (21/20), where "Orythia and Marpesia" are mentioned. Boccaccio names other Amazons as well, but these two appeal to Catherine by their mother-daughter alliance, and by Boccaccio's remark that Orythia was celebrated for her perpetual virginity.

In their use of mythology the Dames des Roches are of course of their time and intellectual milieu, but in their choice and interpretation of mythological figures they have recourse to those whom they can endow with their own particularities, with their "difference." They want to enter, legitimately, the mythological domain, so important for sixteenth century practitioners of poetry, but they want to do it on their own terms. François Rigolot talks about "the revelatory function of myth as signature of each author" (1976, 7). While Ronsard may identify himself by kinship with Apollo, Catherine looks to the Martesia-Otrera duo to transmute the essential bond with her mother onto a mythological plane.

That bond, inseparable from the notions of creative power and freedom, is also expressed by Madeleine's and Catherine's use of the Ceres and Proserpina myth, another mirror image of their own creative bonding, another guarantee of their own intimacy, and a paradigm of poetry as the giving and receiving of life. Madeleine describes Ceres thus: "The blonde Ceres/ Who, bearer of wheat and maker of laws kept/ As much as she could/ Bodies and souls from perishing" (*Œuvres*). While the "bearer-of-wheat" connotation is commonplace for Ceres, the "lawmaker" designation is not. For the Dames des Roches, it signifies the goddess's role as protector of nature's nourishing rhythms and harmonies, whose orderly movements and laws are beneficial both to material and to spiritual human life. Although Ceres (much more than Proserpina) figures a fair amount in the writings of the Pléiade poets, she is imagined there in the one-dimensional role of a goddess of agriculture, not as the mother-of-life who becomes also, therefore, the mother of poetry for the Dames des Roches. It is not surprising that Catherine chose to translate the poem *De Raptu Proserpinae* by the fourth-century Claudian. Claudian's poem tells the story of the abduction and rape of Proserpina by Pluto, and ends with the terrifying spectacle of a desperate Ceres stalking the earth in search of her daughter. In her translation, which is at the same time an adaptation and an interpretation of Claudian's text, Catherine stresses the anguish of Ceres at Proserpina's disappearance, the closeness of mother and daughter, and the cruelty of the abductor whose villainous act disrupts not only the tender harmony between the goddess and her child, but all the bonds of fruitful harmony and order within the natural world. By the changes—elaborations, digressions, contractions—which Catherine imposes on Claudian's poem, she rejects it as an "indifferent" text, and turns it into a text expressive of her own and her mother's difference, of their needs, of their unique creative ideology. The Ceres-Proserpina myth enacts the love between mother and daughter, sign of possible creativity, and the fear of the male invader as disruptor and destroyer.

But the most telling myth is one which Catherine invents, that of "L'Agnodice" in the *Œuvres*. This long narrative poem starts with an introduction of sixty lines, focusing on the theme of "envy," which Catherine describes as a malignant and destructive passion, citing such of its victims as Abel and Socrates. She relates in greatest detail the story of the Athenian Phocion, mentioned by Plutarch, who, unjustly condemned to take poison, died because of Envy, who had hardened his persecutors' hearts against him. In Plutarch's *Lives*, Phocion's remains are buried by his wife, but in Catherine's version his body is piously entombed by a compassionate stranger, a woman who thus attracts to herself and all women the anger of Envy, who vows that "I shall quicken the souls of husbands, who will become the tyrants of their wives, and who, forbidding them books and knowledge will take from them also the strength to live." These opening lines of the myth properly seek to explain why women have been traditionally deprived of learning and writing: because of men's envy.

The theme of envy is a recurrent one in Pléiade poetry, often associated with that of other evils, such as ignorance or the capriciousness of fortune, as threats to the poetic undertaking and to the poets' peace of mind. Emanating from the vulgar ignorant herd, as well as from rival would-be poets and artistically sterile but ambitious courtiers who wish to displace the poets in the favor of the mighty, envy takes place among the scourges of the poet's existence, enumerated by Etienne Jodelle in this fashion: "ignorance, heavy care,/ Burning ambition too,/ Mockery, and mouth-foaming Envy."

For the Dames des Roches, here and in their other mentions of this vice, envy is simply male envy directed towards women of learning. The traditional guardians of the Book would like to defend its access against women. In order to soften that rather harsh indictment of the male sex, Catherine portrays men as being invaded by Envy, and forced by her to behave disgracefully and heartlessly. After this introduction, the text continues:

"As soon as these words were said, Envy slips into the hearts of men who, seeing their wives smart and beautiful, desire to erase from their minds all learning and literature, the most worthy ornaments of beauty, and, by not allowing them to keep that occupation which so pleases them, to take away from them the pleasures in which the soul recreates itself. How cruel it was for Envy to martyrize gentle beauty in that way: the women right away found themselves beset by fevers, weaknesses, and other ailments. But especially the pain of childbirth caused them incredible torments, since they preferred to die rather than, shameless, tell the [male] doctors their debilitating sufferings. The women—what a pity!—did not dare to help one another, they were made to spin. Their husbands, observing their cruel martyrdom, did not leave off from joking and laughing. Maybe they really wanted to have the experience of two wives, and so they did not care to save them. At that time, there was a gentle young lady, made by Heaven beautiful, wise, and subtle, who, full of pity at the sight of so many beautiful faces rapidly engulfed by the greedy tomb, wanted to save them. She hid her twin apples, so that she could study, disguised as a man, because it was forbidden to women to practice the arts, and even to read about them. This young woman, covering also the gold of her blond hair, studied medicine, and became very expert at it. Then, remembering her affection, she wanted to put her good intentions into deeds and heal the sufferings of her poor sisters by the special virtues of flowers, leaves, and roots, especially with an herb picked on the very spot where Glaucus, eating it, from a man became a god. Having made all preparations, the gentle Agnodice presents herself humbly to serve the women, but they, taking her for a boy, refused her help in the strongest terms. One could tell by their scared faces that they feared Agnodice's hands as lustful hands. Agnodice, seeing their great chastity, esteemed them for their virtue, and uncovering her breasts' round white apples, and the beautiful blond tresses of her golden head, showed that she was a girl, and that her gentle heart wanted to deliver them from their sad maladies. The women, admiring her innocent modesty, and the bright white color of her soft skin, and the little twin mounts of her adorable breast, and the beautiful crinkly gold of her blessed head, and the ravishing flames of her divine eyes, and the attractive gracefulness of her sweet words, kissed her mouth and her breast a thousand times, while receiving help from her happy hands. Soon, one could see women and girls recover their fresh skin, and become more beautiful.

But Envy, who was present at this caring enterprise of helping, seeks soon to stop it. She ate out her heart, miserable meat, worthy repast of those she commands, and held in her hand a raging serpent whose cruel venom she spread everywhere. In her other hand she held a thorny branch; her body was leaden, her face full of spite, and around her bald head vipers were wreathed, who kept biting her. Dragging with her a whirlpool of raging furies, she set out to make trouble in honorable marriages, for the peace of another is her unhappiness. She made the men suspect the worth and the gentle graces of the beautiful Agnodice, telling them that their wives and daughters were more taken with Agnodice's beauty than was becoming to women mindful of their honor. The men, inflamed with anger, took Agnodice captive, to make a pitiful sacrifice to Envy. Alas! Without finding her guilty of any misdeed at all, they condemned her unjustly to death. The poor creature, seeing the sad fate awaiting her, quickly uncovered the gold of her blond head, and, showing them her beautiful breasts, pleasant dwelling places of the Muses, of virtue, of grace, of love, she lowered her eyes, filled with shame. A virginal blush rose in her cheeks when she told them that her desire in disguising herself was not to deceive them, but to make it possible for her to study, so that she would be able to serve their wives. And she told them that to suspect her of infamous crimes was an offense against nature and her divine laws. After she had spoken not one voice was raised against her. On the contrary all who were present were amazed at that rare excellence, and they remained filled with wonder, without speaking or moving. Thus one sees, sometimes, after a long storm, the winds die down and the waves become calm, when the twin brothers [i.e., Castor and Pollux], looking out over the sea, and seeing a pitiful ship in danger of sinking, decide to save it from shipwreck, and pluck it from the waves to make it land at the desired shore. So the men, vanquished by pity, appease the furor of their hostility, and, humbly greeting the maiden, ask her forgiveness for their sin. She, who was very happy, begged them urgently to allow the women of the land to study, without envying the glory they would gain by serving Memory's daughters [i.e., the Muses]. Envy, recognizing that her efforts were defeated by the deeds of Agnodice, has ever since persecuted with undying hatred all women as virtuous as she."

Catherine had found the rudimentary plot for this myth in Hyginus's *Fabulae* (third century A.D.), but she so transforms that elementary given into a full-fledged myth that we may really call it her own. In his *Fabulae* 274 entitled "Quis quid invenerit" or "Who invented what," Hyginus gives examples of all sorts of inventors and their products—bits and saddles for horses, the needle, the compass, the trumpet and so on. After his mention of such medical inventors as Chiron, who first used herbs in surgery; Apollo, who first treated illnesses of the eyes; and Asclepius, who first practiced clinical medicine, Hyginus tells of a certain Agnodice, an Athenian virgin, to whom he attributes the invention of obstetrics. Having studied medicine disguised as a man, Agnodice reveals herself to the women who need her, and eventually to the men who had accused her of corrupting their wives. After that last revelation the doctors harass her all the more, but intervention by the leading women of Athens saves her and "the Athenians amended the law, so that free-born women could learn the art of medicine" (1960, 176).

The difference between the Latin embryonic sketch and Catherine's fully formed myth are evident. The main points she retains are those of the threatening hostility of men, and of a woman as a healer of other women, but she transfers both these notions from the limited sphere of physical danger and illness exclusively to the wider sphere where illness is of the soul as well as of the body. The physical suffering is for Catherine not just a metaphor for spiritual pain and decline, it also *is* spiritual travail, as both the body and the soul are caught up in the male-inflicted victimization causing the suffering. Woman's body is used by Catherine as the scene on which male envy and the subsequent deprivation of learning/creativity are enacted. "Like Kafka's victim in 'In the Penal Colony' women have had to experience cultural scripts in their lives by suffering them in their body," remarks Susan Gubar (1985, 299), and this understanding is incorporated already by Catherine des Roches in her myth, as it is in her resolute adoption of chastity—a refusal to suffer inscribing.

That the stifling of creativity undermines both physical and spiritual health is an accepted fact in the latter part of the twentieth century, but it was not when Catherine des Roches formulated it for women in the sixteenth century. Significantly, childbirth becomes an "incredible torment": when creativity becomes impossible, the impossibility includes the creativity of giving birth. Julia Kristeva notes that maternity may favor intellectual and artistic creativity (as it should, since it *is* creativity) if it is able to free women from the imposed rigidity of social and mental structures, and from artificial boundaries between herself and the Other (1977, 6). Maternity is then a joyous delivery/deliverance rather than a grim confinement, as the mother is the active subject of gestation—she *does*, and in doing creates herself and the child—rather than its passive tool or object.

But the women in Catherine's myth have been imprisoned in the deadening routine epitomized by spinning, and severed from joy and energy, from "the pleasure in which the soul recreates itself," and, as importantly, from each other. Catherine extends the life-giving bond between herself and Madeleine to the necessity of a bond among women as indispensable for creativity. Again, she articulates and mythologizes here an insight that certainly had not been expressed in her poetic milieu, and had not been enacted, except maybe in religious communities of scholarly nuns, where all creativity would of course be seen in the light of a higher reason and good. In their illness, the women can be healed only by a woman. Their husbands have become jeering spectators of their miserable lives, and the intervention of the "lustful hands" of men—tools of reification and invasion—can only aggravate the women's powerlessness and isolation, and their debilitating illness. Chastity—the refusal of these threatening hands—is a rejection of alien, destructive intervention in favor of Agnodice's helping and healing practice.

Agnodice's name means "the Unknown"[12] and resounds with significance. Julia Kristeva remarks that "the declaring of the proper name . . . stands for a whole universe of discourse" (1974, 341) and François Rigolot states that "as a rule, the significance of the poetic Name may be perceived as a roundabout way of approaching, indirectly, the ideology of the text" (1976b, 468). "The Unknown" is full of ideological resonances, evoking the idea of women deeply unknown in their intellectual and creative needs and capacities; of women condemned to un-knowing each other and themselves, and so their potential creativity; of women's problematic and often limited access to knowing through learning, only obtained at the price of occulting their female identity; of the danger yet the need inherent in knowing and being known. Agnodice's name is an accusation and a manifesto. It is, in all its resonances, a fitting name for the female Muse she represents.

The physical description of this figure stresses both her erotic and her motherly aspects, not as contradictory, as convention would often have it, but as one. This erotic/maternal joining is clear in the emphasis Catherine places on Agnodice's breasts. The "twin apples" are a sign of bonding with other women in pleasure and nourishment, and in the shared body/mind experience of victimization and of desire: the desire of the forbidden Book, which the mother may restore to her deprived daughters. Vindicating and validating the powerful erotic pleasure of creativity and the maternal urge of giving and nurturing life, Agnodice is the quintessential Muse/healer. As healer she is akin to Apollo, whom Ronsard calls "Poet, and master of all herbs," (1950, Odes 1, 20), and whom he implores for "the strong herb which changed/Glaucus as soon as he ate it, making him immortal," the same herb Agnodice uses to heal the women by admitting them to poetry and immortality. This healing aspect, important but not necessarily dominant in Apollo, is the crucial activity of Agnodice. The meaning is clear: poetry, learning, the Book heal women's deadly alienation from themselves as life-givers and from other women. Through the Book, women may be freed from their destructive imprisonment in an imposed and limited occupation, and find access to life, honor, and poetic immortality.

By setting up a myth of weakness and unknownness on the one hand, and of necessary female bonding and creative healing on the other, "Agnodice" establishes for women an authority of origin that subsumes weakness and danger in an encompassing strength. However, there is a threatening precariousness in the ending of the myth. Agnodice has temporarily subjugated the hostility of men by an apotropaeic gesture of physical and intellectual self-revelation, which, miraculously, calms their anger. The "twin apples" subdue male savagery, much as the twin demigods, Castor and Pollux, tamed the raging sea. It is exactly the "miraculous" (i.e., improbable) character of this event that adds to the ultimate fragility of the myth's ending. Envy will continue to persecute women who, as lovers, sisters, daughters of Agnodice, continue to aspire to learning and poetry.

Catherine des Roches' mythopoeic enterprise, of which Madeleine is, as we have seen, an integral part, has thus resulted in establishing within the poetic institution of the French sixteenth century another institution: that of women poets. Catherine did not, did not want to, and could not consciously want, to establish that new and different program as totally separate from the male one; rather, inside the humanistic tradition of learned poets she has asserted, by the accepted means of mythological authentication, the existence of a female poetic genealogy and power suited to the needs of her gender. Recognizing that "the text is in league with genitality" (Kristeva 1974, 613) and recognizing also the dominant male genitality coded into the important predecessor-texts as well as into the discourse of her contemporaries, she strives to develop a female poetics, justified and illustrated by a female myth leading to a text which, while it is firmly embedded in the dominant male milieu of learned and poetic conventions, is nevertheless a female text. In the Dames des Roches' work and life we see the perpetual pull between their desire to be part of the literary sphere, and their intuition, confirmed by experience, of the basic incongruity of that desire. In "Agnodice" they come closest to inventing an *écriture féminine*, recognizing and incorporating the female body as field and expression of their social and intellectual experience, and keeping in mind the ever-present danger of sociosexual hostility and opposition. They state their ambition while identifying the problems of achieving it.

Elaine Showalter remarks that "the concept of *écriture féminine*, the inscription of the female body and difference in language and text . . . describes a Utopian possibility rather than a literary practice" (1985, 249). For Catherine des Roches and her mother, the Agnodice myth is less the construction of a Utopia than a translation of their closeness, of their work, and of their struggle toward the Book. By allowing them to voice their aspirations and their fears and thus come to terms with them, the myth enables them to claim the right, based on demonstrable necessity, of access to the realm of the Book, and to do this not as the erudite and slightly absurd *femmes savantes* depicted, however admiringly, by their contemporaries, but as lucid and self-conscious poets, eager to conquer, together, the "power to express themselves," as Catherine has formulated it, or, in Madeleine's words, to fix on paper "the word, true image of the soul, and the fugitive voice": the voice of their female Muse.[13]

Notes

1. For an excellent study of the life, milieu, and works of the Dames des Roches, see Diller (1936).

2. Quoted by Diller (1936, 13). For the relations between the Dames des Roches and Scaliger, see Diller (1936) and Grafton (1983).

3. Less a well-constituted and organized group than a list of poets—a list that varied considerably at different times, and included Ronsard, du Bellay, de Baif, and Jodelle as the most frequently cited names—the Pléiade shared certain poetic and linguistic investigations and principles.

4. All quotes from the Dames des Roches are translated by me from the sixteenth century editions, except when otherwise indicated.

5. The "Epistre à sa Mere" from the *Œuvres* was translated by Anne Larsen.

6. In an article entitled "Still Practice, A/Wrested Alphabet: Toward a Feminist Aesthetic," Jane Marcus cites my translation of this sonnet, and comments that "here is a poem by a sixteenth-century Frenchwoman who overcomes her anxiety, as I would argue most modern women writers have, by keeping a hand in both worlds" (1984, 85). I interpret the sonnet in a much less optimistic way. When I read the

translation at a learned gathering, a male poet scathingly commented that "nobody can hold both a pen and a spindle in one hand," meaning this remark as a derisive criticism of the poem, but unwittingly stressing the point Catherine des Roches is making, and putting his finger on the problem of many would-be women writers. For the problem of women's ambivalence toward their various roles, which may cripple women writers, see, for instance, Gilbert and Gubar (1979).

7. Most "ordinary" men too will not conquer individual immortality, but they are included in significant groups and as such play a recognized albeit anonymous role in social, political, economic, and cultural history. Joan Kelly comments on the fact that women, as a group, are invisible in traditional history, and remarks: "Women have been largely excluded from making war, wealth, laws, government, art, and science" (1984, 2), all activities recognized by historians.

8. Translated by Anne Larsen, except for the last words, where Larsen has "to sing their own praise." The French *se chanter elles mesmes*, translated literally, evokes more strongly the self-expressive act writing could and should be for women.

9. Madeleine and Catherine des Roches died in effect on the same day, of the plague that ravaged Poitiers for several months in 1587.

10. An allusion to the gift of fire by which Prometheus made humans superior to animals.

11. Madeleine's second husband seems to have been dearly beloved by his wife and his stepdaughter; both express their grief at his final illness and death in letters and poems. Nevertheless, he remains a shadowy figure in their life, and it is hard to see him as central or even important to their interests and occupations.

12. In "The Trial of Saint Eugenia" (1920) Campbell Bonner suggests that "Agnodice" in the Latin text be amended to "Hagnocide," which he then translates as "chaste before judgment." In his edition of Hyginus' *Fabulae* (1933), H. I. Rose includes that emendation. However, when we see the Greek root of the name not as ἀγνός (*hagnos* or chaste) but as ἀγνώς (*agnos* or unknown), we do not need the emendation, and my translation stands.

13. In this chapter I have incorporated parts of Sankovitch, "Inventing Authority of Origin: The Difficult Enterprise" (1986).

The Dame des Roches: Works Cited

1. *Les Œuvres des Mes-dames des Roches de Poetiers mere et fille*. 1578. Paris: L'Angelier.

2. *Les Œuvres de Mes-dames des Roches de Poetiers mere et fille. Seconde edition, Corrigee et augmentee de la Tragi-comedie de Tobie & autres Œuvres poëtiques.* 1579. Paris: L'Angelier.
3. *Les Secondes Œuvres de Mes-Dames des Roches de Poictiers, Mere & Fille.* 1583. Poitiers: Nicolas Courtoys.
4. *Les Missives de Mes-dames des Roches de Poitiers mere et fille, avec le Ravissement de Proserpine prins du Latin de Clodian: Et autres imitations et meslanges poëtiques.* 1586. Paris: L'Angelier.

Also mentioned in this chapter:

La Puce de Madame des Roches: Qui est un recueil de divers poemes Grecs, Latins, et François, Composez par plusieurs doctes Personnages aux Grands Jours tenus à Poitiers l'an M.D. LXXIX. 1582. Paris: L'Angelier.

For a complete list of manuscripts, and of contemporary and later editions, see Diller (1936). There are no complete modern editions of these works available, and all quotes have been translated from *Les Œuvres* (second edition), *Les Secondes Œuvres,* and *Les Missives.*

Works Cited

Bainton, Roland H. 1980. "Learned Women in the Europe of the Sixteenth Century." In *Beyond Their Sex: Learned Women of the European Past.* Ed. Patricia H. Labalme, 117–28. New York: New York University Press.

Bénouis, Mustapha Kemal. 1976. *Le Dialogue philosophique dans la littérature française du seizième siècle.* The Hague: Mouton.

de Billon, François. (1555) 1970. *Le Fort inexpugnable de l'honneur du sexe Femenin.* New York: Johnson Reprint.

Bonner, Campbell. 1920. "The Trial of Saint Eugenia." *American Journal of Philology* 41: 253–64.

Castor, Grahame. 1964. *Pléiade Poetics.* Cambridge: Cambridge University Press.

Cave, Terence C. 1972. "Ronsard as Apollo: Myth, Poetry and Experience in a Renaissance Sonnet Cycle." *Yale French Studies* 47: 76–89.

———. 1979. *The Cornucopian Text: Problems of Writing in the French Renaissance.* Oxford: Clarendon Press.

Chamard, Henri. 1939. *Histoire de la Pléiade.* Paris: Didier.

Clements, Robert. 1942. *Critical Theory and Practice of the Pléiade.* Cambridge: Harvard University Press.

Daly, Mary. 1978. *Gyn/Ecology: The Metaethics of Radical Feminism.* Boston: Beacon Press.

Demerson, Guy. 1972. *La Mythologie classique dans l'oeuvre de la "Pléiade."* Genève: Droz.

Diller, George E. 1936. *Les Dames des Roches: Etude sur la vie littéraire à Poitiers dans la deuxième moitié du XVIe siècle.* Paris: Droz.

Du Bellay, Joachim. (1549) 1972. *La Deffence et illustration de la langue françoyse.* Paris: Bordas.

———. 1982. *Œuvres Poétiques.* Paris: Nizet.

Du Bois, Page. 1982. *Centaurs and Amazons.* Ann Arbor: University of Michigan Press.

Ferguson, Margaret W. 1983. *Trials of Desire. Renaissance Defenses of Poetry.* New Haven: Yale University Press.

Feugère, Léon. (1860) 1969. *Les Femmes poètes au XVIe siècle.* Genève: Slatkine reprints.

Gilbert, Sandra M., and Susan Gubar. 1979. *The Madwoman in the Attic: The Woman Writer and the Nineteenth-Century Literary Imagination.* New Haven: Yale University Press.

Grafton, Anthony. 1983. *Joseph Scaliger: A Study in the History of Classical Scholarship.* Oxford: Clarendon Press.

Gubar, Susan. 1985. " 'The Blank Page' and the Issues of Female Creativity." In *The New Feminist Criticism.* Ed. Elaine Showalter, 292–313. New York: Pantheon Books.

Heilbrun, Carolyn G. 1979. *Reinventing Womanhood.* New York: Norton.

Homans, Margaret. 1980. *Women Writers and Poetic Identity.* Princeton: Princeton University Press.

Hyginus. 1960. *Fabulae.* Trans. and ed. Mary Grant. University of Kansas Publications in Humanistic Studies, 34. Lawrence: Kansas University Press.

Jodelle, Etienne. 1965–68. *Œuvres Complètes.* 2 vol. Ed. Enea Balmas. Paris: Gallimard.

Keating, L. Clark. 1941. *Studies in the Literary Salon in France 1550–1615.* Cambridge: Harvard University Press.

Kelly, Joan. 1984. *Women, History, and Theory.* Chicago: University of Chicago Press.

Kelso, Ruth. 1956. *Doctrine for the Lady of the Renaissance.* Urbana: University of Illinois Press.

King, Margaret L. 1980. "Book-Lined Cells: Women and Humanism in the Early Italian Renaissance." In *Beyond Their Sex: Learned Women of the European Past.* Ed. Patricia H. Labalme, 66–90. New York: New York University Press.

King, Margaret L., and Albert Rabil, Jr. 1983. *Her Immaculate Hand: Selected Works by and about the Women Humanists of Quattrocento Italy.* Medieval and Renaissance Texts and Studies, 20. Binghamton: Center for Medieval and Early Renaissance Studies.

Kleinbaum, Abby Wettan. 1983. *The War Against the Amazons.* New York: McGraw-Hill.

Kristeva, Julia. 1974. *La Révolution du langage poétique.* Paris: Editions du Seuil.

_____. 1977a. "Maternité selon Giovanni Bellini." *Polylogue,* 409–35. Paris: Editions du Seuil.

_____. 1977b. "Un nouveau type d'intellectuel: le dissident." *Tel Quel* 74: 3–8.

La Croix du Maine, François Grudé, sieur de. (1584, 1585) 1969. *Les Bibliothèques françoises de La Croix du Maine et de Du Verdier.* Gras: Akademischen Druck-u. Verlangsanstalt.

Larsen, Anne R. 1984. "Catherine des Roches' 'Epistre à sa Mere' (1579)." *Allegorica* 9: 58–64.

_____. 1987. "Catherine des Roches 1542–87: Humanism and the Learned Woman." *Journal of the Rocky Mountain Medieval and Renaissance Association.*

MacFarlane, I. D. 1974. *Renaissance France: 1470–1589.* London: Ernest Benn.

Maclean, Ian. 1980. *The Renaissance Notion of Woman.* Cambridge: Cambridge University Press.

Marcus, Jane. 1984. "Still Practice, A/Wrested Alphabet: Toward a Feminist Aesthetic." *Tulsa Studies in Women's Literature* 3: 79–97.

Pasquier, Etienne. (1723) 1971. *Œuvres Complètes.* 2 vols. *Lettres* vol. 2. Genève: Slatkine Reprints.

Pérouse, Gabriel-A. 1977. *Nouvelles Françaises du XVIe siècle.* Genève: Droz.

Rich, Adrienne. 1976. *Of Woman Born.* New York: Norton.

Richardson, Lula McDowell. 1929. *The Forerunners of Feminism in French Literature of the Renaissance: From Christine of Pisa to Marie de Gournay.* Johns Hopkins Studies in Romance Literatures and Languages, 12. Baltimore: Johns Hopkins University Press.

Rigolot, François. 1976a. "Mythologie et Poésie à l'époque de la Pléiade: Problèmes et Méthodes." *Mythology in French Literature. French Literature Series* 3: 1–9.

_____. 1976b. "Rhétorique du nom poétique." *Poétique* 28: 466–83.

———. 1977. *Poétique et Onomastique: L'Exemple de la Renaissance*. Genève: Droz.

———. 1982. *Le Texte de la Renaissance: Des Rhétoriqueurs à Montaigne*. Genève: Droz.

Rogers, Katherine M. 1966. *The Troublesome Helpmate: A History of Misogyny in Literature*. Seattle: University of Washington Press.

Ronsard, Pierre de. 1950. *Œuvres Complètes*. 2 vols. Ed. Gustave Cohen. Paris: Gallimard.

Rose, H. I., ed. 1933. *Hyginus' Fabulae*. Leyden: Sythoff.

Sankovitch, Tilde. 1986. "Inventing Authority of Origin: The Difficult Enterprise." *Women in the Middle Ages and the Renaissance*. Ed. Mary Beth Rose, 227–43. Syracuse: Syracuse University Press.

———. "The Rapt of Proserpina: From Claudian to Catherine des Roches." Unpublished paper.

Showalter, Elaine. 1985. "Feminist Criticism in the Wilderness." In *The New Feminist Criticism*. Ed. Elaine Showalter, 243–70. New York: Pantheon Books.

Spivak, Gayatri. 1981. "French Feminism in an International Frame." *Feminist Readings: French Texts/American Contexts*. Ed. Colette Gaudin et al. *Yale French Studies* 62: 154–84.

Tyrrell, Wm. Blake. 1984. *Amazons: A Study in Athenian Mythmaking*. Baltimore: Johns Hopkins University Press.

PATER FAMVLAM · IPSE · VOLVIT

Prophane, ces Escrits n'ont qu'vn mot à té dire:
Tu n'auraschez GOVRNAY que louër ny que lire.

Portrait of Marie de Gournay by Matheus. Seventeenth century engraving.
Courtesy of the Bibliothèque Nationale, Paris.

⫸ 3 ⫷

ᴏᵛᶜarie le Jars de Gournay

The Self-Portrait of an Androgynous Hero

In the archetypal journey, the hero moves through
frightening ordeals in order to re-create the self.

Ihab Hassan

Androgyny seeks to liberate the individual from
the confines of the appropriate.

Carolyn G. Heilbrun

When a writer invents or adopts a myth as a means of self-
expression, there is necessarily an element of the self-portrait in that
myth. Marie de France's "wildness"—that is, her perception and use
of the crucial difference and marginality implied in her femaleness—
and the Dames des Roches' expression of their desire to conquer
access to the Book and to extend that healing access to all women,
function as keystones of their respective myths, and paint and portray them in very essential ways. Marie de Gournay goes farther
when she makes her autoportrait into her myth and, conversely,
fashions her myth through her autoportrait, effecting a complete coincidence between the two.

Marie de Gournay liked to talk about herself, and has done so
abundantly throughout her works, and more specifically in the following three pieces: "Vie de la demoiselle de Gournay" (Life of the
demoiselle de Gournay), "Apologie de celle qui escrit" (Apology for
she who writes), and "Peincture de Moeurs" (Character-portrait).

The first is a partial autobiography, a description of her family, life, and circumstances up to the time of her return from her pilgrimage, after the death of Michel de Montaigne, to his château and his family; the second is a long, defensive reply to rumors about her eccentricities of thought, behaviour, and domestic management; the third—the subject of this chapter—is a versified self-description that concentrates neither on events nor on self-defense (although elements of this are present), but, as the title indicates, on a definition of herself in terms of her virtues and her vices. We have, then, in these three pieces an autobiography, an auto-apology, and an autoportrait.[1]

The self fascinates Marie as it fascinated her mentor, Montaigne, but while he was intent on its never ending movements and contradictions, on its multiplicities and on the "opaque depths of its innermost folds" (1948, 2:6),[2] Marie—and this is especially clear in the "Peincture"—strives to present herself as a solid, clearly defined, fixed whole, that is, as a creature of myth much more than as a constantly evolving, changing, fundamentally ungraspable and fluid being. Not surprisingly, her mythic context is the epic-heroic one, which allows for the construction of a character that, all in one piece, complete with virtues and vices, confronts a threatening world. In his book on *The Song of Roland*—the Old French epic that will serve as point of comparison to establish the epic coloring of Marie de Gournay's myth of self—Eugene Vance states: "Like the characters of the *Iliad* . . . the characters of *The Song of Roland* enter the poem with an established identity. In contrast with the hero of modern literature, such as Hamlet, Alyosha Karamazov . . . the hero of French epic . . . enters a world of fixed truths with a fixed identity to be tested by the spears and swords of outrageous Fortune. In other words, the unfolding of time in *The Song of Roland* does not bring progressive states of awareness in its hero; it measures instead human *constancy* and not *change*. Roland does not grow qualitatively during his ordeals, but only becomes more like himself as the tale advances" (Vance 1970, 11). As we shall see, this evocation of an epic career applies to Marie's youth, to her becoming, which is a coming-into-herself, and to the mythic description of what she has become.

Marie de Gournay (1565–1645) is best known for her connection with Montaigne, whom she met as a very young woman, and whose editor she became after his death. Although she lived a large part of her long life in the seventeenth century, when the rich, unruly diversity and exuberance of the French Renaissance disappeared into the more austere and "rational" intellectual ambiance of the so-called classical period, she was, as her biographer Marjorie Ilsley has explained, "a true daughter of the Renaissance [since] the burning enthusiasm for learning that permeated the atmosphere of that epoch possessed her from adolescence to old age" (1963, 11).

Eldest daughter of a large, aristocratic family which, especially after the father's death in 1577, was rather impecunious, Marie did indeed pursue learning as an adolescent, and that in the most difficult of circumstances. As an adult she lived her whole life in an ambiance of intellectual stimulation and curiosity, often admired for her erudition and her vast knowledge, acquired with the fervor of the true autodidact, often also cruelly ridiculed and even persecuted for what seemed to be her pedantism and eccentricities. Like Catherine des Roches she did not marry; as the same Etienne Pasquier who had disapprovingly remarked upon Catherine's decision in favor of celibacy says about Marie, "She never proposed to have any other husband than her honor, enriched by the reading of good books" (Pasquier [1723] 1971, 18:1). Since Marie, being not well-off and supposedly rather plain, according to the taste of the time, is not a desirable heiress like Catherine des Roches, Pasquier does not bother to voice social disapproval. Others were to call Marie "an old Sybil" and "a thousand years old virgin" (Ilsley 1963, 159), in the age-old tradition of misogynystic attacks directed toward what in French are called "vieilles filles" and in English "old maids" or "spinsters."[3]

For a long time Marie de Gournay has been mostly studied because of her connection with Montaigne. Léon Feugère is probably the first, in 1860, to consider her as an autonomous presence in literary history, and to recognize her unique accomplishments and qualities. Ilsley's exhaustive biography has, a hundred years later (1963), called renewed and deserved attention to the interest presented by Marie's life, works, and personality. That interest has been sustained through recent explorations focusing on particular aspects of Marie's writings (e.g., Lausberg 1977; Baader 1979; Rowan 1980; Stanton 1983; and Dezon-Jones 1983).

It is undeniable, however, that Montaigne did play a great role in Marie de Gournay's life, especially in her conception of herself and thus in the elaboration of the myth she created of and about herself. The title of "fille d'alliance"—covenant daughter—of Montaigne is one she cherished. Whether she bestowed this title upon herself or Montaigne gave it to her is not entirely clear. It is found in a paragraph at the end of Montaigne's essay "Of Presumption" (1948, 2:17), where we read the following high praise of Marie de Gournay:

> I have taken pleasure in making public in several places the hopes I have for Marie de Gournay le Jars, my covenant daughter, whom I love indeed more than a daughter of my own, and cherish in my retirement and solitude as one of the best parts of my own being. She is the only person I still think about in the world. If youthful promise means anything, her soul will some day be capable of the finest things, among others of perfection in that most sacred kind of friendship which, so we read, her sex has not yet been able to attain. The sincerity and firmness of her character are already sufficient, her affection for me more than superabundant, and such, in short, that it leaves nothing to be desired, unless that her apprehension about my end, in view of my fifty-five years when I met her, would not torment her so cruelly. The judgment she made of the first *Essays*, she a woman, and in this age, and so young, and alone in her district, and the remarkable eagerness with which she loved me and wanted my friendship for a long time, simply through the esteem she formed for me before she had seen me, is a phenomenon very worthy of consideration.

Scholars disagree on the authenticity of the paragraph; some are convinced that it is indeed Montaigne's writing (e.g., Ilsley 1963, 31 n. 20; and Butor 1968, 215–16), while the majority consider it an addition by Marie de Gournay to the 1595 posthumous edition of Montaigne's *Essays*, the first edited by her (e.g., Faguet 1911; Schiff 1910; Frame 1965; and Sayce 1972) and thus "the product of a pious lie of Marie to stress to her contemporaries her role as only authorized and competent editor" (Schiff 1910, 14). Whether Montaigne or Marie wrote the passage, whether it is a vignette-like evocation by Montaigne of his young admirer (their age difference was more than thirty years) or an intercalation into Montaigne's text by Marie, what strikes the reader is the intensity of the feelings of Marie for Montaigne. For *her* feelings are described here, much more than his, and if Marie, as may well be the case, is the author, we must see the paragraph not as an opportunistic lie, but as an attempt to formulate her own hopes for herself, and her deep need of Montaigne as a guarantee of her own potential. By embedding herself, in the form of this paragraph, inside Montaigne's work, she embeds herself in the realm of the Book. When she describes herself as "one of the best parts of my (i.e., Montaigne's) being," she constitutes herself as part of that realm which, more than anything, Montaigne represents for her, and to which she had aspired from her earliest years on. She herself has told the story of her relationship with the famous author in the "Vie," her brief and partial autobiography, told in the third person. Here we read about her desperate efforts, as a young girl, to penetrate into the sphere of learning and literature. Her mother, a widow in charge of a large family, beset by financial worries and steeped in traditional ideas about women's function in society, did not think book-learning essential or even necessary for a girl, and Marie describes how "during mostly stolen hours she studied by herself, and even learned Latin without a grammar and without help, by comparing the Latin books translated into French with the Latin originals. She had to study like that as much because of the aversion her mother felt for such things, as because of the fact that maternal authority had brought her suddenly, after her father's death, to Gournay in Picardy, a spot very far away from all facilities for learning either by teaching or by conversation."[4] She obviously lived in—and suffered from—quasi-total intellectual loneliness and isolation, when, as a girl of fifteen or sixteen, she read Montaigne's *Essays* and "started to desire a meeting with their author more than anything in the world." After the "extreme unhappiness" caused by a false rumor of Montaigne's death, she was able, during a trip to Paris, to meet him finally in 1588. An immediate sympathy sprung up between them, and Montaigne eventually paid several visits to her and her family at Gournay before the end of that year. The "Vie" goes on to tell how, after Montaigne's death (in 1592), his wife and daughter sent Marie Montaigne's working papers, the last revisions of his *Essays*, asking her to take care of a new edition, and inviting her to visit them at the château of Montaigne in Guyenne, which eventually she did, staying with them for fifteen months. The "Vie" then ends with a brief physical description of herself—"she is of medium height, well made, with a light olive complexion, chestnut-colored hair, a round face, neither pretty nor ugly"—and with the promise that she will tell more about herself in a forthcoming poem—an allusion to the "Peincture." The last line contains a reference to her future work "which she is almost ready to bring forth." Her autobiography, written in 1616, ends there with the year 1596, significantly enough: the events that made her have happened, and the announced self-portrait will show what she has become.

Those important events are the meetings with the *Essays* and with Montaigne. They signal her entrance into the world of the Book. Where she had fumbled at the gates, she sees them now thrown open for her. Her inarticulate desire, which had pushed her to persevere with her studies unguided and unencouraged, now blazes into definition and clarity, and it is evident that her desire is for herself as much as for Montaigne. She wants to become actualized in all the possibilities of her ardent nature, and Montaigne will provide the impulse for that coming-into-being of herself. If she calls him "father," it is because he has fathered her own eclosion upon her by the inseminating contact with his book. Susan Gubar describes the artistic activity of certain nineteenth- and twentieth-century women writers as the product of a violation by a male literary authority of the boundaries of the passive woman's self, as the result of "an infusion from a male master" (1985, 302–3). But Montaigne is not that "phallic master" (1985, 303) Gubar pictures as violating and violently penetrating. Rather, he is the passive tool, appropriated by Marie de Gournay for her own single-minded purpose. It is *she* who conceives a desire for him—that is, for the Book he incarnates—and it is *she* who takes possession of the *Essays* in an ecstasy, a trance, of pleasure. She describes in her preface to the edition of his *Essays* how the first reading of this book so excited and enfevered her that her mother made her drink hellebore, a sedative potion (Ilsley 1963, 21). Afterwards it is *she* who aggressively pursues his acquaintance, and, as it were, seduces him into an intense relationship with her—intense, at least, on the part of Marie, who is constructing herself and her future life through her contact with Montaigne. It is clear, from his visits to Gournay and from his family's generous and trusting attitude toward Marie after his death, that Montaigne was far from indifferent to Marie's devotion, and that he appreciated her admiration for his work, but it does seem unlikely that his feelings for her were as powerful as hers for him. Nor should that surprise us, since her need far surpassed his. At most, his need for her was the reaching out of an older man, not so far from death, toward the promise of survival in the zeal and ardor of a young and eager mind, while hers had all the urgency of a new existence striving toward, fighting for, its expression and fulfillment. She comes at the close of his life; he, in every sense, at the beginning of hers.

In one of his essays (1948, 1:14), Montaigne remarks that, in some countries, it is commonplace for people "to wound themselves intentionally to give credit to their word," and he goes on to give several examples, among which we read the following: "I have seen a girl, to show the ardor of her promises, and also her constancy, strike herself, with the bodkin she wore in her hair, four or five lusty stabs in the arm, which broke the skin and made her bleed in good earnest." All editions of the *Essays* done by Marie de Gournay, beginning with the first one of 1595, replace the first words of this example, "I have seen a girl," with the following: "When I came home from those famous Estates of Blois, I had seen a girl in Picardy, a short while before . . ." Clearly destined to identify Marie, whom Montaigne had indeed visited at Gournay in Picardy, in 1588, the same year he attended the Estates General at Blois (Frame 1965, 276–77), these variant lines may well have been written by her, and, if so, they testify to her desire not only to insert herself into Montaigne's text, into the Book, but also to inscribe her body, by identification with Montaigne's nameless "girl," not with the wound inflicted by the phallic master, but with the mark of her own coming-of-age, in a mimicry of ritual initiation. By placing, or rather deplacing this little episode in Picardy, the scene of her early exile and subjection, she expresses, always through the metaphor of the other girl whose vigor and passion she takes to herself, her determination to destroy the semi-ignorant country girl, destined by her mother for a marriage within the provincial nobility and for a domestic rather than for a bookish life. By marking her body and making it bleed she mars the object of exchange a woman's body is supposed to be in the accepted economy of her class, and, as with her initials, designates it as her own, the object and expression of her will alone. No despairing self-mutilation here, no enactment of a victim's helpless bleeding, but the affirmation, in blood freely shed, of "the ardor of her promises, and also her constancy"—to no one but herself.

Her constancy—that epic virtue—is addressed to the self which she intuits she could and should be, and which she has perceived, as Saul perceived Paul on the road to Damascus, in "the light from heaven" (*Acts* 9.3), in the *coup de foudre*, the lightning stroke of her discovery of the *Essays*. Roland Barthes describes the *coup de foudre*, or love at first sight, as "a hypnosis: I am fascinated by an image: at first shaken, electrified, stunned, "paralyzed" as Menon was by Socrates, the model of loved objects, or captivating images, or again converted by an apparition, nothing distinguishing the path of enamoration from the Road to Damascus; subsequently ensnared, held fast, immobilized, nose stuck to the image (the mirror): ([1977] 1978, 189). What promising, seductive image was it that so attracted her as she glimpsed it in Montaigne's Book? None other than the image of herself, not only as a reader, a daring enough vision in her circumstances, but as a writer. The revelation for her is precisely the fact that she may be both.

Her reading experience had been an arduous one so far. In her "Apologie," she elaborates on the scholarly difficulties evoked in her autobiography, describing herself as reading Latin but afraid to speak it for fear of making mistakes, "without Greek, without Hebrew . . . without Logic, Physics, or Metaphysics, without Mathematics or the rest . . .": in other words, without the intellectual *bagage* that must have seemed to her part and parcel of the educated reader's and even more the writer's background. Deprived and isolated, she must have despaired of ever gaining access to the world of books and ideas. This world tantalized her in her father's dusty, little-used—except by her—library at Gournay, where she had groped for an access to the Book during the "stolen hours" when, alone and insecure but determined, she had forced herself to look for that access in the painstaking deciphering of the Latin tomes which, though she had tortuously decoded their vocabulary and their syntax, kept their enigmatic and awesome distance.

In the *Essays*, Montaigne converses with Latin, Greek, Italian authors in an easy intercourse effected through well over a thousand quotations (McKinley 1981; Villey 1908), inviting his reader to participate in those exchanges with the same intense and intimate familiarity he himself demonstrates. His erudition is obviously enormous, but he has absorbed it into the "natural form" he holds out as a promise in the beginning of the work: "It is myself that I portray. My defects will here be read to the life, and also my natural form," (1948, "To the Reader"). For Marie de Gournay this is the promise of a revelation, not only of *his* form but of *hers*, caged for so long in the appearance of a rather peculiar provincial girl with strange intellectual pretentions, but now, thanks to the *coup de foudre* of the *Essays*, to be revealed in the reality of her deepest aspirations. In *The Act of Reading* (1978), Wolfgang Iser remarks: "The significance of the work . . . does not lie in the meaning sealed within the text, but in the fact that that meaning brings out what had previously been sealed within us" (1978, 157). Iser stresses the important distinction between the meaning and the significance of a text. The meaning of Montaigne's *Essays*, this deeply personal text about one being's experience, lies precisely in the presence of Montaigne's unique voice, and the significance of that meaning, for Marie de Gournay, is that she too may have *her* voice and that *her* voice too may be valuable. She too may write. What had been sealed within her, to use Iser's terms, her intellectual and emotional eagerness and energy, her desire to reach beyond the narrow confines of her life to the limitless world of the Book, is brought to light and, in effect, converted into actual existence and eventual experience; that of her own writing.

It is not surprising that Marie's impulse toward writing, made thinkable through Montaigne, should be marked by her youthful experience of female oppression and suppression. Most of her writings are polemic and apologetic, offering either an active fighting stance, or a justification or explanation of her life and work. Her writings are done from "a position of opposition" (Kaplan 1983, 60); they are not meditative or speculative as Montaigne's are. Her repression, followed by her almost miraculous escape and liberation—for, as Ilsley says, it was only by "strange chance [that] this book [i.e., the *Essays*] had made its way to the remote château at Gournay" (1963, 21)—has made her conceive of herself as someone both embattled and compelled to do battle. Her early history of frustration and penury is certainly at the basis of the myth she creates for herself, that of the epic hero confronting a hostile, jeering world. She does not try to imitate Montaigne's writerly stance. The *Essays* serve her less as an inspiration than as an authorization to seek and gain her own voice. The empowering contact they have provided has made it possible for her to become, to be, herself. To complete that process, which is a process of journeying toward the realized self, and of fertile (birth-giving) mythopoeia, she has to disencumber herself of the "real" Montaigne, and to move him to his appointed place in her myth.

In her first published work, "Le Proumenoir de Montaigne" (The walk of Montaigne, 1594) we may see the first still hesitant gesture toward a complete becoming. Written in 1588, immediately after Montaigne's last departure from Gournay, it is a retelling by Marie de Gournay of a story she had told Montaigne, no doubt to entertain him, in the course of a walk in the gardens of Gournay: hence the title. The story itself is based on a text by the contemporary author Claude de Taillemont, taken from his not very successful book *Discours des Champs Faëz* (Tales from the enchanted fields, 1553), which presented itself as a work dedicated "to the honor and exaltation of Love and of Ladies," and was intended to be "feminist" in tenure, but in fact, as Gabriel-A. Pérouse has pointed out, "retains evident traces of an atavistic mentality" (1977, 136).

The story in question tells the pitiful adventures, ending in despair and a bizarre suicide, of a Persian princess who, during her short life, suffers cruel treatment at the hands of men: first of her father, who should have been her protector but instead persuades her to accept exile and a loveless marriage in the name of filial and patriotic duty, and then of her lover, with whom she runs away and who ends up by betraying and abandoning her for another woman. Alinda—as Marie de Gournay calls her—destroys herself, but not before asking forgiveness of her father. In her penetrating article on this short work, Domna C. Stanton sees in the "Proumenoir" and the framing letter on the one hand, an attitude of subjection and abjection towards the "paternal super-ego" (1983, 21) and on the other, a "parricidal effacement of the Father" (1983, 16) through Marie's repression of her male source, Taillemont (whose name she claims to have forgotten), and through "the repeated interruptions of the paternal plot, wherein the 'I' digresses/discourses on various genetic semes" (1983, 16).

The "ambivalence, an unresolved tension between paternal and genetic semes" (1983, 20) which, Stanton suggests, may be seen in the "Proumenoir," will only be fully resolved after Montaigne's death, when Marie is able to absorb him into the mythic function she has assigned to him. In order to give free rein to her own voice she has to efface the "real" Montaigne, just as her "real" father has had to die so that she might come into the legacy of his library, the enticing and frustrating treasure-trove at the hidden heart of her exile at Gournay. Had he lived, her father would probably have spoken with the patriarchal voice her mother, as a dutiful widow, assumes in his stead when she opposes Marie's desire to study. As her "real" father had to die and recede into his library, so her covenant father will have to die so as to recede completely into the Book. Dead, Montaigne joins the "real" father, who had been the first bequeather of the Book, the John the Baptist as it were to Montaigne's fully redemptive figure. Significantly, Marie de Gournay does not publish anything until after Montaigne's death in 1592, although she had sent him the "Proumenoir" in 1588, and would certainly have been happy to publish it around that time (Ilsley 1963, 34). Stanton suggests that her "little book"—as Marie herself calls it—"found no paternal champion" in Montaigne (1983, 23).

After Montaigne's death, Marie de Gournay finds it possible to become her own champion, and to complete, once and for all, her journey toward her constantly pursued and constant self.

Before we look at that epic-heroic, mythic self, as she presents it in the "Peincture," we should look at the role the practice of alchemy played in Marie's life. She obviously became interested in it when, after her devout trip to Guyenne to visit Montaigne's grave, château, and family, and after various other travels, she settled in Paris in 1598. It was an interest condemned in no uncertain terms by her contemporaries, ostentatiously because of the expense involved when her circumstances were already straitened, but also, as Ilsley suggests, because "at the dawn of the seventeenth century only censure greets a woman who meddled in science" (1963, 96).

How to explain Marie's interest in alchemy? It is certainly not gold she is after, as she says in the "Peincture." What then? Betty Jo Dobbs has pointed out in her book, *The Foundations of Newton's Alchemy*, that until well into the seventeenth century, "alchemy had always been composed of two inextricable parts: (1) a secret knowledge or understanding and (2) the labor at the furnace" (1975, 27). Dobbs goes on to give the Jungian interpretation of this binarity, according to which "these two sides of alchemy really were inextricable, for the secret knowledge about transformation was in reality an unconscious or semi-conscious understanding of certain psychological changes *internal* to the adept. Since he was unaware of their true nature, however, the alchemist projected the process of change upon matter" (Dobbs 1975, 27). The alchemical process is analogous to the process of individuation, that is, "a drive towards wholeness and maturity in the human psyche" (Dobbs 1975, 29), toward the formation of "a new center . . . the 'self' [in which] many pairs of psychic opposites strike a new balance" (Dobbs 1975, 30). It is likely that Marie de Gournay, poring over her crucibles, curious, as she says, about "what will become of the substance I hold over the fire" (Ilsley 1963, 95), was enacting or reenacting the process of her own becoming as, held over the fires of exile from and then of reintegration into the Book, of alienation and then of salvation, she achieves the transmutation into the self whose promise, like that of the philosopher's stone, the *Essays* had held out to her. The alchemical process fascinated her by its implied affirmation that fundamental change is possible, that "blackness"—the blackness of her youthful struggle—will be followed "by its transformation into something new" (Dobbs 1975, 30). It is the new self—a *whole* self—we read of in the "Peincture," mythified into the epic-heroic shape that confers upon that self the necessary qualifications for the battle she wants her writing life to be.

The "Peincture" or autoportrait consists of 164 lines, alexandrines, and may be divided into four sections: an introduction (8 lines), the self-portrait, divided between a description of her vices (46 lines) and of her virtues (108 lines), and a brief conclusion (2 lines).

The introduction sets the stage for the portrait proper: "Espaignet, who are made according to a wiser century,/ I want to paint my character, and to give you that portrait./ You may, as you like, approve it or destroy it,/ Since I have known you for twenty years./ Our acquaintance started when the great Montaigne's/ Tomb I went to see, and to visit his wife and his daughter./ I traveled with you who were accompanying/ Your wife to their [i.e., the Montaigne family's] province, the cradle of your own ancestors" (lines 1–8).

Jean d'Espaignet (1564–1637), a former president of the Bordeaux parliament, and a friend of Montaigne, was traveling back from Paris to Guyenne with his wife, and it was a stroke of good luck for Marie that she was able to join their no doubt well-escorted party.[5] In a time of civil turmoil and religious war, when the countryside was being ravaged constantly by marauding, pillaging troops and their followers, and the roads were full of violence and danger, such a trip was no mean enterprise. Etienne Pasquier, in the letter already quoted, tells how Marie de Gournay "crossed practically the whole of France." He comments: "It makes really a memorable story. The life of this gentleman [i.e., Montaigne] could not have been concluded on a more beautiful *catastrophe* than this" ([1723] 1971: 18:1). *Catastrophe* must be translated as "ending," but the overtones of that particular term are clearly dramatic, theatrical (Huguet 1925–67), and indicate that Pasquier was well aware of the extraordinary character of the feat undertaken by Marie de Gournay, a feat well in keeping with her penchant for the heroic and the grand in life as well as in literature, where "she preferred heroic and epic verse with their color and splendor" (Ilsley 1963, 148). The ending of Montaigne's life constitutes indeed the beginning of the "Peincture."

Marie dedicates her poem to Jean d'Espaignet because he is a link with Montaigne, not only through their friendship, but through Espaignet's belonging to "a wiser century," namely that of Montaigne, himself changed into his tomb, his monument. In a later version of the "Peincture," Marie changes lines 5 and 6 into: "Our acquaintance started when I went to Montaigne/ To see a dead demigod, his daughter and his wife," with "demigod" as a designation for Montaigne, emphasizing the mythifying tendency of this piece. At the end of her 1594 book, which contains the "Proumenoir," she includes a series of quatrains on Montaigne and his family, and here already, immediately after Montaigne's death, we see the same myth-making process taking place. In a quatrain addressed to Montaigne's mother, Marie compares her to Latona, mother of Apollo and Artemis, and says that "she [i.e., Latona] gave birth only to the sun of the heavens,/ And you gave us the nourishing sun of souls [i.e., Montaigne]." In the last quatrain, "to the very illustrious name of Montaigne," she writes: "O name, you end my book/ And you began it too./ So all things start and end/ With the great Jupiter."

The mythification process, it is very evident, started early, and applies both to Montaigne and to his time. To both she attributes perfections Montaigne did not claim either for himself or for his age. Indeed, the essence of his self-portrait consists of a mixture of the preponderance of the self, and the conscience of that self as a flickering, changeable, infinitely interesting, infinitely imperfect thing, and he describes his century as a period of chaos and of intellectual and moral weakness. Of course, we see here the typical process of epic mythopoeia at work. The author of *The Song of Roland*, in the eleventh century, reaches back to a lost, long-ago and therefore "mythologizable" time and ideal—the eighth century of Charlemagne and his knights—in order to galvanize his own age for the growth and the changes in which Western Europe was becoming increasingly, bewilderingly, involved because of the "enlargement of the physical and intellectual boundaries of Western Christendom" (Southern 1953, 219). In the same way, Marie de Gournay distances Montaigne and the sixteenth century, transforming them into a perfect idol and a golden time, empowering her to face the perils, challenges, and changes of her age with courage and even audacity. In his book on the autoportrait, Michel Beaujour notes that "the auto-portrait is haunted by the fantasma of a happy city," and, like Utopia, is built "around an absent structure: vanished places, broken harmonies" (1980, 22). The same may be said about an epic like *The Song of Roland;* it may be seen as an ideological Utopia, inspired by the triple ideology of Christianity, nationalism, and knighthood, and constructed around a largely imaginary Roncevaux and an at least partly fictitious Charlemagne.[6] Montaigne himself looked in his *Essays* to lost, better times and places—the Bresil of the Tupinamba, the Greece of classical antiquity—and to vanished heros, "figures of human achievement" (Nakam 1983, 183): Alexander, Alcibiades, and Socrates most of all.

For Marie de Gournay, the falsification she imposes on the past is less an effect of nostalgia than of her need to create a stable mythic background for her own character. Loss and deprivation are built into that character, but since she now attributes them to the fact of the irretrievably vanished past, she is able to transcend the loss and deprivation of her childhood banishment at Gournay and to give them epic dimensions, just as her blind childhood rebellion against her mother's dictates, and her obstinate, lonely groping toward knowledge are transcended into her mythic character's heroic appetite for struggle and conflict. Early in her life, the pattern of dispossession and resistance has been set, and when Montaigne dies she is able to mythify that pattern into one of epic-heroic proportions. Like Charlemagne, Montaigne recedes into the mists of an impossibly glorious past, while his deathless image, fabricated by Marie, presides reproachfully over an imperfect present, and exacts from his "daughter" a heroism that will make her worthy of him, that is of his tomb, his myth, his incarnation as Book. Marie's self-portrait is therefore haunted less by a "happy city" than by, in Beaujour's words, "the fantasma of a happy city." She is not nostalgic for Gournay, where she had walked with Montaigne but which remains for her a place of enslavement; her "happy city" is less a reality than a stage-set for her autofabrication, her self-made myth: a place evoked as in code in the "Peincture" by "the great Montaigne's tomb."

Against this background Marie will not ask herself, as *autoportraitistes* typically do, "Who am I?" but will state, "Here is who I am, what I am, and against whom I am." We recognize the "whole" stance of the archetypal epic hero, of Roland at Roncevaux, who has no doubts concerning the fundamental rightness and integrity of his being.

Before we examine the body of the "Peincture," we should look at the causes that engaged Marie's interest and combativeness during her long writing career. In various essays she speaks out against slander, envy, false devotion, hypocrisy, the lack of moral grandeur and integrity that she deplores in many of her contemporaries, disrespect for learning and for the life of the intellect, imperfect friendship, and what she calls "grimaces mondaines" (i.e., affectation in manners), but also against the fake values of society, the courtly milieu, unworthy clergy, and a variety of other ills and evils. She values integrity above all other qualities, and sees it as the synonym of goodness, in the full Platonic sense of the word, inseparable from greatness: "Man is good or he is not great." But on two subjects she expresses herself repeatedly and with particular intensity: the condition of women, and the state of the French language.

A champion of women's rights, she states her views principally in two essays, "Egalité des Hommes et des Femmes" (Equality of men and women) and "Grief des Dames" (Women's grievance). She sees men and women as basically equal, and attributes women's so-called inferiority to the faulty education they generally receive, so that "her primary goal is equal instruction for everyone of both sexes" (Insdorf 1977, 61). Notes of anger and indignation at the treatment of women sound strong in her feminist writings, especially in "Grief des Dames." The first lines of this piece—and indeed most of it—express great bitterness: "Happy are you, reader, if you do not belong to that sex to which all good is forbidden, since it is forbidden freedom. And more, it [i.e., the female sex] is not allowed most virtues, since women do not have the power to form such virtues, so that their sole happiness, their sovereign unique virtues are: to be ignorant, to act as fools, and to serve." She feels cruelly the disdain accorded women by even inferior men: "Even if women had the powerful arguments of a Carneades, there is no man so puny who does not snub them with the approval of most of the people present, when, with a mere smile, or a small shake of his head, his mute eloquence says: It's a woman who speaks." Recognized today as an important figure in the history of feminism (Richardson 1929; Ilsley 1963; Stanton 1983), Marie "persistently defied the custom of her time in order to preserve her right to live a life free from the shackles of old conventions, a life devoted to the calling of her choice. She thus became one of the rare professional women writers of her time, espousing causes that were judged inappropriate for women to defend" (Ilsley 1963, 279).

Besides feminism, her other great "cause" was the defense and preservation of the French language of the sixteenth century: the language of Montaigne, of course, but also of other writers of the Renaissance she profoundly admired for their prose, such as Amyot, or for their poetry, such as Ronsard. In this, she takes up the cudgels against seventeenth-century theorists, led by Malherbe, and against their emphasis on poetic technique, on a sparser, more pared-down vocabulary, on what they see as a new simplicity and purity of French syntax and lexicon, on the need to "fix" the language. Against them she defends the importance of inspiration, the need for a rich, various, ever fluid, and expanding vocabulary, the use of synonyms and diminutives, and such elements of poetic style as metaphor and dissonance.

Peggy Holmes calls Marie de Gournay "a critic of unusual sensibility" (1954, 122) and "a writer whose undoubted talents as a critic have been too long ignored" (1954, 129), while Domna Stanton labels her, "the most scholarly female critic before De Stael" (1983, 11). Heinrich Lausberg sees in the opposition between Marie and the Malherbe faction an expression of the age-old conflict, the dialectic tension between *ingenium* and *judicium* (1977, 124). In the latter—the claims of sane and measured rationality—Marie must have recognized the danger of a certain linguistic and intellectual rigidity, of a willful impoverishment of the language, and of a constraint imposed upon its dynamic vitality and vigour. She has been accused, both by her contemporaries and by later critics, of *passéisme*, of a sterile obsession with a past time and a past language. Ferdinand Brunot calls her "the eternal representative of superannuated ideas . . . three times comical in her role of spinster, of pedant, and of ghost from another century" (1891, 556), while Paul Bonnefon comments that "she was always peculiarly behind the times, and soon she made on everybody the impression of a sort of representative of the fashions and the ways of the past" (1898, 2:316). In fact, the opposite is true. It is not only the language of the "wiser century" she defends, but a French idiom full of spirit, inventiveness, mobility, and rich diversity, at a moment when a plethora of rules and interdictions seems to threaten these qualities, which she sees as the best aspects of the French language, to be preserved and championed through all ages.

If such are her causes, who are her enemies, since "the enemy" is as indispensable an element of the epic-heroic myth as "the cause"? Throughout her life Marie de Gournay met with admiration and generosity, even from many whose ideas differed from hers, but also with persistent ridicule, criticism, and even vicious slanderous attacks on the part of those who, in the Parisian social and intellectual milieu, condemned automatically any woman who dared to write, and to write, moreover, on controversial subjects and in an original, self-assured manner. Guez de Balzac, her contemporary, wrote in one of his letters that "I have long declared myself opposed to this pedantry of the opposite sex, and I have said that I would much prefer a woman with a beard than a woman who acts learned . . . Really, if I were a police officer, I'd send spinning all women who want to write books" (Ilsley 1963, 127).[7] Spinning again! Marie herself remarks in her essay on "Egalité des Hommes et des Femmes" that "it's not enough for some people to prefer the male sex to women, but they also want to confine women, by an unshakable and unavoidable decree, to the spindle and to the spindle only." But worse than a generalized misogyny, worse than the pranks and jokes at her expense (of which Ilsley recounts a few, 166–69), worse than the hoax which led her to write her autobiography—when three young men thought it would be amusing to make her believe that King James the First of England had heard of her and desired such a document for his collection of lives of famous women and men (Ilsley 1963, 126)—worse than all these was the satire published when she entered the debate on the causes of King Henry the Fourth's assassination. The Jesuits had been censured on this occasion, and Marie took up their defense, an unpopular and unconventional stand to take.[8] The result was the anonymous pamphlet, the "Anti-Gournay," which dragged her good name through the mud and provoked a spate of grotesque stories about her in which she was caricatured and ridiculed without mercy by often anonymous members of the "establishment" of her time, a male establishment where her femaleness made her a prime victim: as Ilsley says, "she refused to fit into the narrow categories laid down by convention as the only legitimate places in society for a woman of her rank" (1963, 279).

All these experiences help explain her need to create, in her "Peincture," the figure of a heroic character, able to withstand through integrity and courage the attacks of hostile forces.

The body of the "Peincture" comprises Marie's description of her virtues and vices. Beaujour notes that "the autoportrait combines the irreconcilable, vices and virtues which combat each other: psychomachia" (1980, 25), but, as we shall see, there is no sense of interior combat, no déchirement in Marie de Gournay. Her sense of herself, as her sense of values, is epic, and her vices are part of her virtues. Their description is abruptly introduced: "Here then are my flaws." If there is a confessional element here it is free from any repentance, as Marie accepts and even approves of her "flaws," which essentially fall in three categories. The first two are reminiscent of the vices of the epic hero, and are therefore to be admired rather than despised. First, she describes herself as impatient, quick to anger, and of a passionate, impulsive disposition that leads her to trust others ("since I suppose my fellow-creatures to have a conscience like mine") and, often, to experience betrayal by them. She also has a perhaps exaggerated sense of honor, which may cause her to "esteem myself a bit too much," but "who does not see her own virtues does not see her vices." The third category concerns her relative indifference to God: "In serving great God my soul is too cold:/ Although my heart honors Him with a saintly respect." Mitigated by the "although" clause, and justifiable on the grounds of human impotence—"what other mortal can ever adore Him sufficiently?" she asks—this "vice" is hardly described as a serious moral blemish. In any case, the reader understands that God is not relevant to Marie's self-description, his place having been usurped by the "demigod," Montaigne. Her myth is a totally secular one.

The epic-heroic stance prevails: her faults are mainly the result of that impetuousness so typical of the epic hero (cf. Roland) and of her generous desire for honor. Moreover, her shortcomings are justified by the assaults of her enemies (as we have seen, an indispensable epic element) described in this section as "le mondain" (the worlding), "les rieurs" (the laughers), "le siècle trop aveugle" (this too blind age), and "le vulgaire" (the vulgar herd).

In the next section, Marie de Gournay introduces her virtues just as abruptly: "My good qualities will take their place here." At first reading, the lines that follow offer a pell-mell assortment of sometimes contradictory virtues (such as prudence-spontaneity), positively ("I am . . .") or negatively ("I am not . . .") presented. The lines ending this apparently haphazard enumeration offer, however, a clue as to its internal organization: "Equity and candor I have from nature:/ Order I have gained from time and reading." Innate vs. acquired virtues: this is the taxonomic principle that allows us to make sense of the list.

Under the first classification, "equity" holds the first rank, and is mentioned repeatedly: "the laws of equity I embrace with a holy respect; at no price would I let the equity of my life be stained." Equity means for Marie de Gournay the sure sense of right and wrong, which again is characteristic of the epic hero, as is candor, the openness and uncalculating spontaneity which, together with equity, guide her opinions, her judgments, and her actions. Half of Marie's

virtues are variations on these two qualities: her capacity for individual judgment ("I don't judge about anything according to popular
custom"), her undaunted courage ("the assaults of my unhappiness
do not break my courage"), her disinterest in money and luxury ("I
don't like money, except for my needs only"), her total integrity ("I
am very truthful and completely of good faith"), her straightforward-
ness ("I have a noble and frank heart, and I hate all pretence"), her
loyalty ("my promise of friendship is inviolable:/ In good fortune, in
disgrace, in life and in death"), her generosity ("I dispensed my ser-
vices with a full and large hand"); all are epic-heroic traits.

The other half, the acquired virtues, are manifestations of temperament tamed, of order imposed, of spontaneity graciously chan-
neled: her evenness and discretion of moods and behaviour ("my
character and my mood shine with equanimity"), her moderation
and lucidity of judgment ("I do see the vice which mars a friend"),
her avoidance of exaggerated, whimsical, or bizarre actions and
thoughts ("there is no room for capriciousness in my character./ All
that's bizarre I chase to the Indies"), her prudence in the giving and
receiving of advice ("I know to accept counsel meekly"), her assidu-
ity to duty ("I am careful, active, constant in my goals").

Her enemies figure again in this section, both as vices alien to
her (such as "the shameful mud-pit of prevarication") and in the
guise of "the Courts," "the mighty ones," or "the pestilential flat-
terer," all of whom she accuses of vainglory, greed, despicable ambition, and, most of all, of servility and un-straightforwardness: "I
reject the grimaces and the paint of the Court:/ I hate its apishness,
in which all follow one another." Her criticism of the court milieu, a
constant in her writings, has been compared with that of La Bruyère
in his *Caractères* (Baader 1979). This particular dislike may be explained by the fact that the milieu epitomized what she saw as the
sad decadence of manners, morals, and language in the seventeenth
century. In the "Peincture," her enemies offend her moral principles
by their depravity, and, by contrast, lend greater splendor to her own
qualities. Even in her "vices" she has nothing in common with them.
Moreover, the enemies are also accused of taking advantage of her
powerlessness and her poverty ("Oh! How easily is the name of the
poor person oppressed!"), and of treating her with "malice or disdain." Both as passive and as active antagonists, they serve to empha-
size the dangers besieging her, and her alienation from the
corruption surrounding her.

Between her vices and her virtues there is no antagonism but rather complimentarity. The enemy is outside, never inside. The order imposed on her generous temperament is not a feat of hard-won victory over an evil self, but an enhancement of the heroic self.

The final section of the "Peincture" is very brief: "I have seen the final seals placed on this order [i.e., her character],/ Since seven lustra have lapsed since I came of age." Faguet (1911) suggests correctly that "by her coming-of-age Melle de Gournay means her fifteenth or sixteenth year," and that consequently the "Peincture" was written when she was about fifty, which agrees with the indication that twenty years had lapsed since her adventurous trip to Montaigne's birthplace. Since Montaigne's first *Essays* (Books 1 and 2) were published in 1580, and since Marie de Gournay was one of their early and most enthusiastic readers, it is likely that she dates her coming-of-age from that galvanizing discovery, as we have already seen. The "Peincture" ends, then, where it began: with the image of Montaigne, contained in the allusion to her age and to the crucial discovery of the Book.

In his studies of the seventeenth century self-portrait, Jean Rousset evokes the difficulties of the genre: "From the moment the self contemplates itself, it becomes a dangerous labyrinth; in exploring itself the self discovers only a dark underside in which it loses itself without grasping anything" (1969, 544). Elsewhere he repeats the same idea: "To look into oneself is to plunge into half-light or illusion, to go into the labyrinth. There is a tragic side to introspection which is at the same time necessary and impossible, and which God alone can resolve, since he is the only one to see the depth of the human being in its transparency" (1965, 211). Michel Beaujour, in a commentary on Rousset's studies, remarks that they help to explain why "the seventeenth century offers no autonomous self-portrait, which might be situated between the autoportrait as society game and the religious or metaphysical meditation in which the empirical self transcends itself" (1980, 61). Neither society game nor religious meditation, the "Peincture" is a noteworthy exception. Marie de Gournay avoids the difficulties of introspection and the tragic trap described by Rousset by her deliberate adoption of an anachronistic and unfashionable stance, that of the epic-heroic character, and by a transcendence, not towards a hidden God, but towards the familiar/ superior Montaigne/Book. The *mise-en-scène* against the backdrop of the dead idol and the vanished golden age; the conception of self-description as a categorical and categorized enumeration of moral qualities rather than as a labor of introspection; the absence of inner conflict and the presence of outer foes; the traces also of a quasi-feudal language ("to give and receive my law") and the emphasis on honor all contribute to the epic-heroic ambiance. So does the paratactic structure of the piece with its abrupt transitions and its two main parts, each enumerating, with variants, essentially the same characteristics of the hero, much like epic *laisses similaires* echoing and reinforcing each other. For the figure of the labyrinth Marie substitutes that of the joust: the knight (Marie) paying heroic tribute to the liege (Montaigne/Book), in the presence of the witness (Espaignet) and of the adversary (the Court, the Age).

With our modern predilection for the complex, self-analyzing character, we may feel that a certain simplification, or oversimplification, a certain schematisation, results from that choice of conception and style. Marie's interest lies not in self-analysis, but in self-invention and self-structuring, even at the cost of a certain self-simplification.

Marie de Gournay applies the same process of simplification to her body: the only reference she makes in the "Peincture" to her exterior appearance is to describe "my roundness in appearance and in effect," that is, in the reality of the character she evokes. Elsewhere she writes to a friend: "Our two minds are round, and also our two faces," and, as we have seen, in her autobiography she also mentions her "round face." Roundness is for her a spiritual as well as a physical quality. To Marie's spherical appearance corresponds her spherical being: the conformation of her face and body express her longing for the wholeness of the self, archetypically symbolized by the circle and the sphere. In alchemy, the circle is seen as a sign of microcosmic and macrocosmic synthesis. So, for instance, in his *Atalanta Fugiens* ([1617] 1969), the German alchemist Michael Maier includes a particularly suggestive emblem depicting a man and a woman enclosed in a circle, which is in turn enclosed in a square, which is enclosed in a triangle, which is surrounded by a large circle. The accompanying Latin explication reads: "Make a circle out of a man and a woman, and from that a square, then a triangle, and then make a circle and you will have the Philosopher's Stone" (Maier [1617] 1969, 180–81). Jean d'Espaignet knew Maier's emblem book and was particularly

impressed by the engravings (Maier [1619] 1969, 362), and he may
have described this particular emblem to Marie, if she did not see it
herself. In any case, with her interest in alchemy she must have seen
similar images, uniting within the roundness of a circle male and
female in a suggestion of androgyny.[9] As a reader of Plato (whom she
quotes in her feminist writings) she may also have thought of the
description, in the *Symposium*, of the primeval human being, the androgyne, as round.

   This reminds us that the author's gender is not once mentioned
in the "Peincture." Were it not for the feminist adjectival forms, we
would not know whether a man or a woman is speaking: there is no
reference to Marie's womanhood. She presents herself as an androgynous hero, that is, as hero rather than man or woman. This corresponds to her expressed feminist ideal of the whole human being, the
spiritual and intellectual androgyne. In "Egalité" she declares that
"the human animal is neither man or woman, strictly speaking, since
the sexes [i.e., the physical differences between the sexes] are destined only for procreation . . . Nothing resembles a male cat on a
window sill more than a female cat. Man and woman are one." As
Mary Rowan remarks, "she projects her arguments [in defense of
women] consistently onto an intellectualized androgynous plane"
(1980, 278). But the ideal of androgyny—the transcendence of sexual
stereotypes and sex-specific values, and of the establishment of a sex-
neutral standard of human development and possibility (Warren
1982)—originates in her own experience. Carolyn Heilbrun notes that
"androgyny seeks to liberate the individual from the confines of the
appropriate" (1964, 10), and is that not exactly the point of all Marie's
endeavors, liberation from those confines? Society's sex-specific
views of what is appropriate and inappropriate for her as a female
have made her suffer since her childhood and throughout her life,
and would, if possible, have kept her from the Book forever. Across
the centuries, Marie de Gournay agrees with Virginia Woolf, whose
Orlando rejects the sex-role system, "for it meant conventionality,
meant slavery, meant deceit" (Morgan 1972, 191).

   Marie de Gournay wrote her "Peincture," her self-portrait,
when she was fifty years old, at the mid-point of her professional
career. The myth of the epic androgynous hero she created for herself
allowed her to look back on her past battles, and forward to the
coming ones, with a sense of justification and rightness. It allowed

her to surmount the humiliations, great and small, she has endured, and to transcend the petty but painful persecutions her femaleness calls down upon her. Through her myth, she is able to escape from the smallness of her enemies and the limits of her gender, as in her childhood she escaped her mother's call to girlish duties, into the world of the Book. For Marie de Gournay that has always been an embattled world, especially for women, and it is no wonder that she dons heroic-androgynous armor to lay siege to it over and over again, to stake her claims to it, and to conquer it, triumphantly, through the power of her transforming, healing, mythic imagination, and personality.

Notes

1. Elyane Dezon-Jones has studied the echoes and overlaps that link these three pieces in what she sees as an almost palimpsestic relationship.

2. All quotes from Montaigne's *Essays* are taken from *The Complete Essays of Montaigne*, trans. Donald M. Frame.

3. Feminist writers such as Mary Daly have recuperated this term, and have valorized the basic freedom and strength of the Spinsters, whom Daly represents as figures who "counter the main current of phallocracy" (1978, 392).

4. All translations of quotes from Marie de Gournay's works are by me, unless otherwise indicated.

5. Jean d'Espaignet had retired from administration and, not incidentally for his friendship with Marie de Gournay, was engaged in the serious study of alchemy and physics, producing a book (1623) which Betty Jo Dobbs calls "not really alchemical at all . . . a rational statement of Neoplatonic physical theory" (1975, 37).

6. Although scholars do not necessarily agree on the genesis of *The Song of Roland* as a literary work, most do agree that while there is a historical kernel at the work's core, the events and the characters involved have undergone essential transformations in the *Song*. On the historicity and ahistoricity of *The Song of Roland*, see Aebischer 1967; Menéndez-Pidal 1959; Moignet 1957; and Vance 1970.

7. Ilsley gives this quote and translates Balzac's "j'enverrais filer" as "I would drive away." I have altered her translation because of the more appropriate and meaningful use, in this context, of "filer" in its first meaning of "to spin."

8. For an account of this episode, see Ilsley (1963, 106–21).

9. For the figure of the androgyne in connection with alchemy, see Trinick.

Marie de Gournay: Works Cited

Marie de Gournay's collected works were published in *L'Ombre* (Paris: Jean Libert, 1626), and in the expanded and revised *Les Advis ou Les Presens* (Paris: Toussainct Du-Bray, 1634, and Paris: Jean Du-Bray, 1641). Modern editions are not available, although excerpts have been published separately, such as the feminist essays "Egalité des Hommes et des Femmes" and "Grief des Dames" as well as the "Peincture de Moeurs" in Schiff's book. The "Vie de la Damoiselle de Gournay" is included in Dezon-Jones. For a complete list of Marie de Gournay's publications and correspondence, as well as of her editions of Montaigne's *Essays*, see Isley's Bibliography.

Works Cited

Abensour, Léon. 1923. *La Femme et le féminisme avant la révolution*. Paris: Leroux.

Aebischer, Paul. 1967. *Rolandiana et Oliveriana*. Genève: Droz.

Baader, Renate. 1979. "Streitbar und unzeitgemäss: die Moralistik der Marie de Gournay." In *Die Französische Autorin vom Mittelalter bis zum Gegenwart*. Ed. Renate Baader and Dietmar Fricke. Wiesbaden: Athenaion.

Balzac, Jean-Louis de Guez de. 1854. *Œuvres*. 2 vols. Ed. L. Moreau. Paris: Lecoffre.

Barthes, Roland. (1977) 1978. *A Lover's Discourse*. Trans. Richard Howard. New York: Hill and Wang.

Beaujour, Michel. 1980. *Miroirs d'encre: Rhétorique de l'autoportrait*. Paris: Editions du Seuil.

Boase, Alan M. 1935. *The Fortunes of Montaigne*. London: Methuen.

Bonnefon, Paul. 1898. *Montaigne et ses amis*. 2 vols. Paris: Armand Colin.

Brunot, Ferdinand. 1891. *La Doctrine de Malherbe d'après son commentaire sur Desportes*. Paris: Masson.

Butor, Michel. 1968. *Essais sur les Essais*. Paris: Gallimard.

Chevalier, Jean and Alain Gheerbrant. 1969. *Dictionnaire des Symboles*. Paris: Robert Laffont.

Cook, Ellen Piel. 1985. *Psychological Androgyny*. New York: Pergamon Press.

Coudert, Allison. 1980. *Alchemy: The Philosopher's Stone.* Boulder: Shambhale Publications.

Daly, Mary, 1978. *Gyn/Ecology: The Metaethics of Radical Feminism.* Boston: Beacon Press.

Day, Martin S. 1984. *The Many Meanings of Myth.* Lanham, MD.: University Press of America.

Dezon-Jones, Elyane. 1983. "Marie de Gournay: Le je/u/ palimpseste." *L'Esprit Créateur* 23.2: 26–36.

Dobbs, Betty Jo Teeter. 1975. *The Foundations of Newton's Alchemy.* Cambridge: Cambridge University Press.

Faguet, Emile. 1911. "Mademoiselle de Gournay." *Revue des Deux Mondes* 5: 290–301.

Feugère, Léon. (1860) 1969. *Les Femmes poètes au XVIe siècle.* Genève: Slatkine Reprints.

Frame, Donald M. 1965. *Montaigne: A Biography.* New York: Harcourt, Brace and World.

Gubar, Susan. 1985. " 'The Blank Page' and the Issues of Female Creativity." In *New Feminist Criticism.* Ed. Elaine Showalter, 292–313. New York: Pantheon Books.

Heilbrun, Carolyn G. 1964. *Toward a Recognition of Androgyny.* New York: Norton.

Holmes, Peggy. 1954. "Melle de Gournay's Defence of Baroque Imagery." *French Studies* 8: 122–31.

Huguet, Edmond. 1925–67. *Dictionnaire de la langue française du seizième siècle.* Paris: Champion (vols. 1–2) and Didier (vols. 3–7).

Ilsley, Marjorie Henry. 1963. *A Daughter of the Renaissance: Marie le Jars de Gournay, Her Life and Works.* The Hague: Mouton.

Insdorf, Cecile. 1977. *Montaigne and Feminism.* North Carolina Studies in the Romance Languages and Literatures, 194. Chapel Hill: University of North Carolina Press.

Iser, Wolfgang. 1978. *The Act of Reading: A Theory of Aesthetic Response.* Baltimore: Johns Hopkins University Press.

Jung, Carl Gustav. 1972. *Psychologie und Alchemie.* Freiburg im Breisgau: Walter-Verlag.

Kaplan, Cora. 1983. "Speaking/Writing/Feminism." In *On Gender and Writing.* Ed. Michelene Wandor, 51–61. London: Pandora Press.

Lausberg, Heinrich. 1977. "Marie de Gournay et la crise du langage poétique." In *Critique et création littéraires en France au XVIIe siècle,* 117–25. Paris: CNRF.

McKinley, Mary B. 1981. *Words in a Corner: Studies in Montaigne's Latin Quotations.* French Forum Monographs, 26. Lexington: French Forum.

Maclean, Ian. 1977. *Woman Triumphant: Feminism in French Literature 1610–1652.* Oxford: Clarendon Press.

Maier, Michael. 1969. *Atalante Fugitive.* Trans. Etienne Perrot. Paris: Librairie de Médicis.

Menéndez-Pidal, Ramon. 1959. *La Chanson de Roland y el neotradicionalismo.* Madrid: Espasa-Calpe.

Moignet, Gérard. 1957. *La Chanson de Roland.* Paris: Bordas.

de Montaigne, Michel Eyquem. 1948. *Essays.* Trans. Donald M. Frame. Stanford: Stanford University Press.

Morgan, Ellen. 1972. "Humanbecoming: Form and Focus on the Neo-Feminist Novel." In *Images of Women in Fiction.* Ed. Susan Koppelman Cornillon. Bowling Green: Bowling Green University Popular Press.

Nakam, Géralde. 1983. "Figures et espaces du rêve dans les *Essais.*" In *Montaigne et les Essais.* Ed. Pierre Michel. Actes du Congrès de Bordeaux (1980). Paris: Champion.

Ong, Walter J. 1981. *Fighting for Life: Contest, Sexuality, and Consciousness.* Ithaca: Cornell University Press.

Pasquier, Etienne. (1723) 1971. *Œuvres Complètes.* 2 vols. *Lettres* vol. 2. Genève: Slatkine Reprints.

Pérouse, Gabriel-A. 1977. *Nouvelles Françaises du XVIe siècle.* Genève: Droz.

Richardson, Lula McDowell. 1928. *The Forerunners of Feminism in French Literature of the Renaissance: From Christine of Pisa to Marie de Gournay.* Johns Hopkins Studies in Romance Literatures and Languages, 12. Baltimore: Johns Hopkins University Press.

Rousset, Jean. 1965. "Monologue et soliloque (1650–1700)." *Ideen and Formen. Festschrift für Hugo Friedrich,* 203–13. Frankfurt: Klostermann.

———. 1969. "Les Difficultés de l'autoportrait." *Revue d'histoire littéraire de la France* 69: 540–50.

Rowan, Mary M. 1980. "Seventeenth-Century French Feminism: Two Opposing Attitudes." *International Journal of Women's Studies* 3: 273–91.

Sayce, R. A. 1972. *The Essays of Montaigne: A Critical Exploration.* Evanston: Northwestern University Press.

Schiff, Mario. 1910. *Marie de Gournay.* Paris: Honoré Champion.

Southern, R. W. 1953. *The Making of the Middle Ages.* New Haven: Yale University Press.

Stanton, Domna C. 1983. "Woman as Object and Subject of Exchange: Marie de Gournay's *Le Proumenoir* (1594)." *Esprit Créateur* 23.2: 9–25.

———. 1985. "Autogynography: The Case of Marie de Gournay's 'Apologie pour celle qui escrit'." *Autobiography in French Literature. French Literature Series* 12: 18–31.

Tideman, L. E. 1903. "The Friends of Montaigne." *Westminster Review* 159: 29–39.

Trinick, John. 1967. *The Fire-Tried Stone.* London: Stuart and Watkins.

Vance, Eugene. 1970. *Reading the Song of Roland.* Englewood Cliffs, N.J.: Prentice Hall.

Villey, Pierre. 1908. *Les Sources et l'évolution des Essais de Montaigne.* 2 vols. Paris: Hachette.

Warren, Mary Anne. 1982. "Is Androgyny the Answer to Sexual Stereotyping?" *"Femininity," "Masculinity," and "Androgyny."* Ed. Mary Vetterling-Braggin. Totowa, N.J.: Rowman and Allanheld.

Simone de Beauvoir. 1945. By permission of Robert Doisneau, Photo Researchers, New York, New York.

❧ 4 ❧

Simone de Beauvoir

The Giant, the Scapegoat, the Quester

> In the final analysis, the prerogative of autobiography consists in this: that it shows us not the objective stages of a career ... but that it reveals instead the effort of a creator to give the meaning of his own mythic tale.
>
> Georges Gusdorf

One of the best known, if not *the* best known, of twentieth-century French women writers, Simone de Beauvoir (1908–86) has produced a vast body of work, consisting of philosophical, political, and sociopolitical essays; travel accounts; novels; short stories; a play; and a great number of autobiographical writings which include, besides the four parts of her autobiography, a short work on the death of her mother, and an account of Jean-Paul Sartre's last years.[1] Almost everyone is to some degree familiar with her political and feminist activities and opinions. Her rejection of her upper-middle-class background in favour of a life of the intellect and of *engagement*; her long and "open" relationship with Sartre; her wide-ranging travels; her affairs with Nelson Algren and Claude Lanzmann; her connection with the ideology and the cultural phenomenon of existentialism; all have become part of the quasi-legendary *persona* whose strong presence has marked the post-World War II French, and to a certain degree, the international intellectual scene. Her impact may have been felt most in the area of contemporary feminism, although critics disagree on the precise nature and extent of the influence exercised by *The Second Sex*. That the book met with—and continues to enjoy—widespread international success is indisputable. As Anne Whitmarsh says: "Simone de Beauvoir is a cult figure and her book compulsory reading, a sort of bible for supporters of the women's movement" (1981, 152). Until her death, women involved in feminist militancy, interested in different aspects of the female experience, or simply fascinated by the personality of Simone de Beauvoir, continued to make pilgrimages to her Paris apartment, as to a shrine of feminism.

If we are better acquainted with the details of this author's life and thoughts than with those of most writers, male or female, it is because she has written about herself very extensively.

The four volumes of Simone de Beauvoir's autobiography (*Mémoires d'une jeune fille rangée; La Force de l'âge; La Force des choses; Tout Compte fait*)[2] may well be described by applying Philippe Lejeune's definition of the genre as "a retrospective account in prose that a real person makes of his own existence, stressing his individual life and especially the history of his personality" (1975, 14). Lejeune goes on to pinpoint all the elements in this definition needing further examination, and states that it is indispensable that the author, the narrator, and the *personnage* of the autobiography be identical (15). In Simone de Beauvoir's case, the coincidence of identities is never in doubt; she affirms it in the strongest possible terms and by all means, such as the constant use of the first person singular, and the numerous mentions of the one proper name to indicate all aspects of the triple writing/telling/living activity. The presence and the force of the *one* personality revealed in this complex activity pervade and dominate all four volumes of the autobiography.

There are, as it were, two vertical structural lines running through the successive books; the story of herself, and, parallel and often entwined with it, the story of her time. In the first volume, the first structural line is much the stronger and that fact makes the *Memoirs*, as most critics agree, the most interesting of the four volumes. This book involves the greatest amount of self-recreation, and Simone de Beauvoir obviously tackles it with great gusto.

Lejeune talks about the "autobiographical pact" which autobiographers conclude with their readers, often in a preface or at the start of the work, in which the author profers, as it were, "a sort of birth certificate of his discourse" (1971, 72). In this "rite of presentation" (72) are stated the choices and decisions the author has made concerning the register, the voice, the mode of discourse which are to follow. Lejeune notes that, at the beginning of the *Memoirs*, there is no such autobiographical pact, but that "in the following volumes Simone de Beauvoir returns to a more natural attitude: each volume is preceded by a pact in the proper required form, which develops the traditional autobiographical discourse" (1971, 80).

In the preface to the second volume, however, Simone de Beauvoir does in fact give a *post facto* "birth certificate" to the first one in this interesting paragraph:

> I had long wanted to set down the story of my first twenty years; nor did I ever forget the distress signals which my adolescent self sent out to the older woman who was afterwards to absorb me, body and soul. Nothing, I feared, would survive of that girl, not so much as a pinch of ashes. I [i.e., the adolescent "I"] begged her successor [i.e., the adult "I"] to recall my youthful ghost, one day, from the limbo to which it had been consigned. Perhaps the only reason for writing my books was to make the fulfillment of this longstanding prayer possible. When I was fifty, it seemed to me that the time had come. I took that child and that adolescent girl, both so long given up for lost in the depths of the unrecalled past, and endowed them with my adult awareness. I gave them a new existence—in black and white, on sheets of paper" (*Prime of Life* [1960] 1962, 9).

The dialogue between the past and the present (in the guises of the adolescent and the adult self) takes on the structure of a claim, with the past as claimant and the present as debtor. The adolescent self is imagined/recalled by Simone de Beauvoir as conscious of the debt the future adult self is piling up with her, as she (the adolescent) is presented as conscious of bearing the embryo of the becoming adult self. This debt, then, is no more or less than Beauvoir's life, such as it has turned out to be, in its precise shape and exact configurations of writer, thinker, public person, private being—and especially of writer. As the young self gave birth to the adult one, so the latter will now resurrect—through writing—and give a "new existence" to the former, in order to "discharge a debt" (*Prime of Life*, 10). Simone de Beauvoir, in other words, will tell her own genesis precisely because it was and is her genesis, and, as such, inseparable from her present self. She undertakes an archaeology not so much of her past life as of her past self, which is the foundation, the keystone, of the present one: buried maybe, but nevertheless a necessary and integral part of the edifice that has risen upon it. The past, to carry the metaphor a little farther, is the dust, the earth in which the keystone is embedded and hidden, and its importance lies only in the artifact it surrounds. We might call the *Memoirs* (which cover the years 1908–29) an almost Proustian undertaking, but while Proust makes present and past inseparable and mutually redemptive, Simone de Beauvoir lays out the past—the dust—as being very much behind her, cast off, and captured in its rejected past-ness rather than in its eternity. Only the self, indestructible, marches on. The life is told because of the self.

In the same preface, Simone de Beauvoir justifies her autobiographical undertaking *in toto* on the basis that readers like to understand the nature of writing: where it comes from, in what situation it occurs, by whom it is done and how. The first volume is then the story of "how my vocation as a writer was acquired" (*Prime of Life*, 10), which makes it especially important for our examination of the woman writer's access to the Book. The problem of self-cognition in the re-creation of a much younger self is solved by Beauvoir by lending, as she says, "her adult awareness" (*Prime of Life*, 9) the consciousness of a fifty-year-old woman, to the disappeared child and adolescent, thereby stating a unity of the self that abolishes for her what has been called the "epistemological dilemma" (Renza 1980, 275) of the autobiographer. She posits a continuity of the self firmly anchored in one continuously informing experience, the experience of the writer, which, in the first volume, is the experience of being a becoming, a *called* writer.

Simone de Beauvoir treats with great seriousness the notion of "calling" that Sartre so ruthlessly savages in *his* autobiography, *Les Mots*. Her calling is strongly connected with her desire for autonomy and supremacy ("I was, and I would always remain, my own master," *Memoirs* (Beauvoir [1958] 1974, 59), with her early awareness of purpose and goal ("*my* life is going to lead somewhere," 104), and with her strong sense of her own identity ("I was not 'a child': I was me, myself," 60), all inseparable notions present throughout the *Memoirs*. From the first paragraph on, she identifies and poses herself as a first-born: "As far back as I can remember, I was always proud of being the elder: of being first" (*Memoirs*, 5) and that premise of pride, privilege, and superiority is persistently present. The child

Simone wants to become a writer, because she admires writers, and "was convinced of their supremacy" (*Memoirs*, 141).

She herself has been deeply touched by many writers. Through Maggie Tulliver, over whose fate she weeps bitter tears, she identifies herself with George Eliot: "One day other adolescents would bathe with their tears a novel in which I would tell my own sad story" (*Memoirs*, 140); through Ménalque in *Les Nourritures Terrestres* she uses Gide's revolt against the family to give conviction to her own rebellion: " 'Family, I hate you! You dead homes and shut doors!' Ménalque's imprecation reassured me that by finding home dull I was serving a sacred cause" (*Memoirs*, 194). The life of the Book—of scholars, writers, thinkers, teachers—appeals to her because it seems to promise the possibility of affecting others, of playing a role in their lives, of dominating. Dominance is her deepest ambition: "I raised my eyes and looked at the oak tree: it dominated the landscape and there was not another like it. That, I decided, is what *I* would be like" (*Memoirs*, 141). More than any other profession or vocation the writer's work would allow her both to escape from the limits of her social and familial background and to make her mark on others. By being a writer, she could obtain the autonomy she desired: "I wanted to be a law unto myself; I now thought that literature would allow me to realize this dream" (*Memoirs*, 141). It would also give her the authority she craved: "I aspired . . . to play the leading roles in life" (*Memoirs*, 88). Autonomy and authority are the components of her envisioned supremacy.

The pursuit of supremacy is an important structural element in the *Memoirs*, forming the pattern of her relationship with others and of her attitude toward the ideas her parents and her milieu would like to impose upon her. The drive toward supremacy empowers her to shape these relationships (or to escape from them) and to fight against these ideas. Her childish fantasies of being a victim like Genoveva of Brabant or a martyr like Joan of Arc or Saint Blandine; of being Jo in *Little Women* "superior to her sisters" (*Memoirs*, 90) or Maggie Tulliver in *Mill on the Floss*; her curiosities about literature, sex, "the world outside"; and her darkest preoccupations (with death, with annihilation) all reflect her drive toward supremacy, toward the affirmation of herself as "the One and Only" (59), different and ultimately separated from her family and milieu. In all these instances of fantasy, curiosity, or fear she evinces a wish to be the focus, the center, of attention: if not of others, at least of her own.

What happens to her—in reality, in fear, or in imagination—is uniquely important. "Only Simone de Beauvoir really dies" (Marks 1973, 55), writes Elaine Marks to indicate the author's constant need to affirm the supremacy of her own personality throughout all its experiences. In a family whose demanding affections as well as stern rules threaten to abolish her, this "egotism" (Marks 1973, 127) is needed to counter "my most obsessive worry: how to defend myself against other people" (*Memoirs*, 192), and to allow her progress along the vertical line of the self, steadily rising to supremacy, as Simone de Beauvoir accedes to "my own freedom," the free self she mentions in the last line of the book.

Robert Cottrell defines the *Memoirs* as "essentially the story of the author's transcendence [of her parents' world of immanence], consistently presented as an exemplary rejection of the bourgeois values that dominate her parents' world" (1975, 9). It was a world in which the Book was reduced to acceptable books, part of a carefully screened and selected set of artifacts called "culture." These artifacts, situated in the domains of music, literature, and the visual arts (cinema being excluded as "vulgar entertainment," Cottrell 1975, 53), scrupulously acquired, each at its appointed time, and sanctified by a long history of approval and canonization, testified to the good taste and the impeccable education of the upper middle class. In this perspective, the Book is constantly mutilated and distorted through the application of censure and selection based on tradition and convention.

When Simone was a small child, her mother was pleased to take out a subscription to the Bibliothèque Cardinale—a "safe" lending library on the Place Saint-Sulpice—for her clever little daughter, and to assist her in selecting "appropriate" books from the catalog, but when books became the all-important reality in the adolescent girl's life ("the only reality within my reach," as she says) then the situation changed as far as books were concerned: "my parents cast black looks upon them" (187). Simone's rejection of *their* authors (Anatole France, Guy de Maupassant) in favor of *hers* (Gide, Proust) caused increasingly severe disagreements, as they called her chosen books "pretentious, oversubtle, queer, decadent and immoral" (*Memoirs*, 187).

But the conflict between Simone and her parents concerns not only her free access to reading, but, indirectly and more importantly, her eventual access to free writing; that is, for Simone de Beauvoir, writing against her milieu, against everything she englobes under the words "the bourgeois status" (*Memoirs*, 218). For this—the ultimate access to the Book—Beauvoir needs to shed all the traditional views, prejudices, attitudes, and often cherished attachments of her childhood environment, and the *Memoirs* are precisely the story of that shedding. Each shedding in this process, while it may be painful, is also marked by a small or large feeling of intellectual contempt, which makes it possible for Simone to jettison her attachments. One by one she casts them off: her teachers at the Cours Désir, such as the Abbé Trécourt, and afterwards those at the Institute Sainte-Marie, where Mademoiselle Lambert who at first "filled me with respect" (*Memoirs*, 173) later "no longer interested me" (288), and where her initial appreciation of the talented Robert Garric "died at the same time as my faith in his work" (225); her parents, cousins, aunts—all her family; friends who, having at first intrigued and interested her become quickly disappointing and dull; and God himself, who is not very different from any other friend, uncle, or teacher, his main function having been to confirm Simone's sense of herself and her uniqueness. When her confessor, Abbé Martin, commits the gaffe of speaking to her with the voice of her "church-hens" of teachers, God shares in his disgrace: "Perhaps God was stupid!" (*Memoirs*, 135). It takes not much more than that contemptuous suspicion to sweep him out of her life: "I realized that He was playing no further part in my life, and so I concluded that he had ceased to exist for me" (*Memoirs*, 137).

She talks several times about her need for an *alter ego*, but the *alter ego* is "a humble vassal" (*Memoirs*, 60): a submitted being in the case of her sister, and clearly a weaker creature in the case of her friend Zaza, in spite of the admiration Simone professes to feel for her. It is only at the end of the book that in Sartre she finds her perfect twin, "the double in whom I found all my burning aspiration raised to the pitch of incandescence" (*Memoirs*, 345). He talks to her about herself and validates her sense of herself: "We used to talk about all kinds of things, but especially about a subject which interested me above all others: myself. Whenever other people made attempts to analyze me, they did so from the standpoint of their own little worlds, and this used to exasperate me. But Sartre always tried to see me as part of my own scheme of things, to understand me in the light of my own set of values and attitudes" (*Memoirs*, 340). Sartre will not be shed. Here the question of supremacy ends, in a shared supremacy.

In this exploration of growing up/ affirming supremacy, Simone de Beauvoir proceeds very systematically, moved always by the impulse, or the compulsion, to explain. Typically, the vertical line of her self-development is punctuated by units of experience offered in three parts: narration, discussion, conclusion. She narrates a small event—collecting money for "the poor little Belgian refugees" (*Memoirs*, 27) during World War I, for instance, or her first communion—then explains and discusses what that event or experience meant to her, or rather what it had given her in terms of gratification, pleasure, pain, or humiliation, and concludes by stating the resulting short- or long-term impact on her existence and on her notion of herself. Each of these small instances has a metonymical effect, as it signals a larger pattern: the narration of her childhood, its dissection and examination, and the conclusion, when the self separates itself from its cage.

The second vertical line, the story of her time, is thus represented in this book by echoes of events, such as World War I and its attendant manifestations of patriotism, all of which are absorbed in Simone de Beauvoir's drive toward supremacy, and by lists of books, ballets, plays, and films functioning as signposts to Simone's development. "I remained indifferent to the great events which were taking place in the world" (*Memoirs*, 237), she remarks, but the fact that she is in a state of gestation excuses that indifference as it also explains her hesitations about sex. Both the violence of the world and the possible violence of sex, which she juxtaposes, terrify her at the same time that they do not really involve her: "It was not I but the world that was at stake: if men had bodies that were heavy and racked with lust, the world was not the place I had thought it was. Poverty, crime, oppression, war: I was afforded confused glimpses of perspectives that terrified me" (*Memoirs*, 291). Her contacts with both violence and sex are still only those of an observer, even if they come sometimes dangerously close to hurting her physically. When as a student at the Sorbonne she allows strange men to accost her and sometimes pick her up in bars, on the street, or in pinball parlors, she is obviously playing with fire, but these are not encounters which engage her sexuality: they merely satisfy her curiosity, even when she sometimes has to conclude that "I'd really had a fright" (*Mem-*

oirs, 172). Her very terrors confirm her supremacy as they suggest the willfulness and the intensity of her gestation, and the eventual intensity and magnificence of her self-accomplishment.

Underlying the vertical structure of her self-development, and supporting it, we read in Simone de Beauvoir's *Memoirs* a secret horizontal mythic structure, intersecting the vertical and interacting with it at all points as subtext with text. This mythic structure, hidden yet visible (as the figures in a game of "find the hidden pictures"), consists of three mythic tales which are, as it were, subterraneously present throughout the *Memoirs:* the tale of the Giant, the tale of the Scapegoat, and the tale of the Quester.

The myth of the Giant is embedded in the *Memoirs* in the form of Rabelaisian evocations of vitality and energy, often expressed in terms of eating. Gargantua and Pantagruel, the giants whom Rabelais made into optimistic incarnations of the possibilities of Renaissance humanity, are characterized by their hugeness—of appetites, of endeavors, of conquests. They eat, they study, they laugh, they fight— all prodigiously. In the thirty-second chapter of *Pantagruel,* Rabelais constructs a whole world—complete with mountain ranges, forests, meadows, cities, countries, people—in his giant's mouth. Just as in Hindu mythology Krishna's mother, Devaki, sees in the mouth of her son all the worlds revolving and realizes that he is the Lord of the Universe, so Rabelais allows us to witness in Pantagruel's mouth humanity's discovery of new worlds, "with all the astonishment, the widening horizons and change in world picture, which follow upon such a discovery" (Auerbach (1946) 1957, 236).

The small Simone also possesses the world through her mouth: "The world became more intimately part of me when it entered through my mouth than through my eyes and my sense of touch" (*Memoirs,* 6). When her parents give a party, "I would crack between my teeth the candied shell of an artificial fruit, and a burst of light would illuminate my palate with a taste of black-currant or pineapple: all the colours, all the lights were mine, the gauzy scarves, the diamonds, the laces; I held the whole party in my mouth" (*Memoirs,* 17). Eating is an act of possession, of power: "I was never attracted to paradises flowing with milk and honey, but I envied Hansel and Gretel their gingerbread house: if only the universe we inhabit were completely edible, I used to think, what power would we have over it!" For Simone "eating was not only an exploration and an act of conquest . . . but almost my most solemn duty" (*Memoirs,* 7).

Simone de Beauvoir demonstrates, throughout her work, a strong awareness of death, as Elaine Marks has convincingly shown in her book on the subject, and death is present in the *Memoirs* as well: Louise's baby dies; so do several older members of Simone's family, and Zaza Mabille, her dearest friend. More importantly, the child—and the young girl—has intimations of her own death. She fears "all the separations, the refusals, the desertions to come, and . . . the long succession of my various deaths". But these fears may be countered by the continuous drive to power: "I went on eating all the same" (*Memoirs*, 8). Eating means growing, both literally and figuratively, and growing is desirable as it leads to autonomy and strength. The bigness of others is scary, but may be countered by becoming big oneself. Surrounded by big, matronly women, "I felt the same terror as Gulliver did when the young giantesses displayed their breasts to him" (*Memoirs*, 100), but Gulliver visits the land of Lilliput as well as Brobdingnag, and it is as a giant that Simone de Beauvoir emerges from *her* travels through childhood and adolescence.[3] Afraid of being absorbed by her family and milieu, of "being swallowed alive" (*Memoirs*, 52), she will instead be the one who does the swallowing, as she increasingly sees the whole world as edible: "I wanted to crunch flowering almond trees, and take bites out of the rainbow nougat of the sunset. Against the night sky of New York, the neon signs appeared to me like giant sweetmeats" (*Memoirs*, 7). Books too are like candy. She describes "a dozen volumes bound in paper covers whose colours were as sharp and fresh as those of boiled sweets: pistachio green Montherlant, a strawberry red Cocteau, lemon yellow Barrès, Claudels and Valéry in snowy white" (*Memoirs*, 186). She devours and possesses them, as she hungrily devours and appropriates all experiences that come her way. Striding through Paris, as Gargantua had done, she observes and absorbs greedily, taking in all the smells, sights, and sounds with an almost gluttonous avidity, feeling herself at the center, the core, of an immense pulsing maelstrom of inchoate energy and fascinating, rich, nourishing life:

> I would visit all the exhibitions, and go for long prowls round the galleries of the Louvre. I would wander all over Paris, my eyes no longer brimming with tears, but looking at everything. I loved those evenings when, after dinner, I would set out alone

on the Métro and travel right to the other side of Paris, near Les Buttes Chaumont, which smelt of damp and greenery. Often I would walk home. In the boulevard de la Chapelle, under the steel girders of the overhead railway, women would be waiting for customers; men would come staggering out of brightly lit bistros; the fronts of cinemas would be ablaze with posters. I could feel life all round me, an enormous, ever-present confusion. I would stride along, feeling its thick breath blow in my face. And I would say to myself that after all life is worth living" (*Memoirs*, 241).

She burns with the desire to conquer that world through discovery and exploration. Like Gargantua she leaves one education behind—the Cours Désir, the Institute Sainte Marie—to accede to another which will free her, as Gargantua was freed, for continuing conquest. Her vigor and her vitality are impetuous and immoderate, and justify as well as explain her need to go beyond the narrow boundaries of her milieu. In an article significantly entitled "Simone de Beauvoir: l'incessante conquête," Elène Cliche has analysed the importance of the notion of conquest, which she calls "an open word, a catalyst of active, spontaneous . . . liberating forces" (1984, 25) in the work of Simone de Beauvoir. She traces the presence and the impact of that notion and all its implications in Beauvoir's essays (beginning with *Pour une morale de l'ambiguïté*) as well as in her novels and in her autobiography.

The mythic tale of the Giant—or Giantess—valorizes Beauvoir's "voracious desire to conquer [the world], to absorb it" (Cliche 1984, 37), and justifies her drive toward supremacy, at the same time that it wards off some of the anxieties and guilt the ruthlessness of that drive must engender. Gigantism renders nonsupremacy impossible, and Simone-as-giant must fulfill her destiny.

The mythic tale of the Scapegoat is one she herself refers to (without naming it) when she remembers a childhood book, André Laurie's *Schoolboy in Athens*, and retells the story of two young friends, the serious, painstaking, rather plodding Theagenus, and the brilliant, charming, artistic Euphorion. Euphorion dies young, while Theagenus lives to write about the two of them. Beauvoir comments: "I identified Zaza with the handsome blond ephebe and myself with Theagenus" (*Memoirs*, 113), and indeed Zaza dies young, and fifty years later—exactly like Theagenus—Simone de Beauvoir writes their story. Implicit in this little tale is the idea that one dies so the other might live and be creative, an implication Beauvoir renders explicit in the last line of the *Memoirs:* "I believed that I had paid for my own freedom with her death" (360). Simone ends up "owning the universe" (*Memoirs*, 114) while Zaza dies, sacrificed to the bourgeois family and value structure against which she had fought in vain.

Elizabeth Mabille, Simone's schoolmate and friend, belonged to a family which, actively Catholic and socially as well as financially superior to Simone's, was even more staid, strict, and conventional. Intolerant of everything that threatened or seemed critical of their status and traditions, they looked askance at Zaza's intellectual and artistic aspirations, and increasingly, as both girls grew into young women, at her friendship with Simone: "It was under my influence that Zaza preferred studying to domestic life, and I was lending her scandalous books" (*Memoirs*, 309), but also "I realized that the Mabilles and their friends didn't think much of me . . . in their eyes I was heading for an ignominious future" (*Memoirs*, 255–56).

When Zaza falls in love with Jean Pradelle, who is Simone's friend but also "from an excellent family . . . and a practising Catholic" (*Memoirs*, 333), Simone dares to hope her dearest friend will be happy after all, but the hesitations and the scruples of Pradelle, fearing to upset his widowed mother by an engagement, and the subsequent opposition by the Mabilles to the relationship, cause in Zaza "deadly struggles" (355) which exhaust and weaken her. Soon she becomes gravely ill: "she had a high temperature and frightful pains in the head" (*Memoirs*, 358). After a few days she dies in the clinic at Saint-Cloud where her doctor had had her moved, and it is there that Simone sees Zaza for a last time: "She was laid on a bier surrounded by candles and flowers. She was wearing a long nightdress of rough cloth. Her hair had grown, and now hung stiffly round a yellow face that was so thin, I hardly recognized her. The hands with their long, pale fingernails were folded on the crucifix, and seemed as fragile as a mummy's" (*Memoirs*, 360). In Simone's eyes this is the icon of a dead martyr, of a sacrificial victim, of a scapegoat.

The figure of the scapegoat or surrogate victim is, as René Girard remarks, that of "an ideal educator . . . in the etymological sense of *e-ducatio*, a leading out" ([1971] 1977, 306). Just as the rite of the surrogate victim allows others "to escape their own violence . . . and bestows on them all the institutions and beliefs that define their

SIMONE DE BEAUVOIR   113

humanity" (Girard 1977, 206), so the death of Zaza leads Simone away from "the revolting fate that had lain ahead of us" (*Memoirs*, 360) and into a fully human world of freedom and openness. Elaine Marks stresses how crucial Zaza's death was for Simone's later development: "It . . . became with time the symbol of all of Simone de Beauvoir's formative years. Her revolt against church and family, her passionate hatred of the bourgeoisie, and her exacerbated sense of responsibility seem to have crystallized around this death. Had Zaza not died it is possible to imagine that Simone de Beauvoir would not have carried with her, after her adolescent liberation, such strong feelings of revolt" (Marks 1973, 51). Without Zaza's dying, Simone's efforts toward growth might have been stunted, left incomplete; she might not have "gotten out" as completely as she did. She quotes Zaza's last words to her mother: "There are outcasts in all families; I'm the outcast in ours" (*Memoirs*, 359). But if Zaza had been able to accept the status of outcast, she might have lived. She was not ruthless enough to cast off the bonds tying her to her mother especially, and to the conventions of her class. Her death, however, allows her friend to embrace the position of triumphant, voluntary outcast vis-à-vis that suffocating, closed world, and to be cast out into a wide open world. Already, before Zaza's death, Simone had been able to feel herself "no longer . . . rejected by my environment; it was I who had rejected it in order to enter that society . . . in which all those minds that are interested in finding out the truth communicate with each other across the distance of space and time" (*Memoirs*, 283), and Zaza's disappearance sets the final seal on that undertaking of freedom.

The sacrifice of a victim implies a process of identification with that victim, as well as an essential dis-identification. Simone and Zaza shared many of their aspirations, interests, and desires, but Zaza, however gifted, had none of Simone's relentless drive toward intellectual and personal affirmation of superiority and autonomy. Her passionate tenderness, her inability to hurt the very people who encage her and who would impose upon her an excruciating "atrophy of the heart and the mind" (*Memoirs*, 328), her scruples and her delicacy, which Simone scathingly calls her "high-mindedness" (356), all these traits constitute the fatal weakness which designates her, and not Simone, as a sacrificial victim.

Zaza's death, as told by Beauvoir, has something mysterious about it, in that the precise medical cause of death is not clear. As Konrad Bieber remarks: "The author leaves it undecided whether the

extreme emotional pressure that Zaza was subjected to had anything
to do with her death or whether it was a clinical case" (1979, 40), and
Elaine Marks is absolutely correct in saying that "the nature of Zaza's
malady is incidental. What matters is that she died and that her
friend survived" (1973, 54). It is this survival-bought-by-death structure of the event (as interpreted by Simone de Beauvoir) that confers
upon that event—Zaza's untimely death—its sacrificial and mythic
character.[4]

But Zaza is not the only scapegoat Beauvoir meets along her
climb toward supremacy—all sacrificed to the evils she escapes from.
Among them are fairy tale figures such as Andersen's little mermaid,
mentioned twice in the Memoirs (48, 51), sacrificed for her innocent
passion: "she had not done anything wrong: her tortures and her
death made me sick at heart" (51); and real-life figures such as Guite
Larivière, Zaza's mother, who eventually serves as the main accom-
plice in her daughter's destruction, but who had been a sacrificed girl
herself: "impulsive, vivacious, beautiful," at a young age she had
been pressured by her family to make a "good" but to her deeply
unsatisfactory marriage (115), and had become a discontented but
conventional matron, ending up, after abandoning her youthful
dreams, as a "perfect specimen of her bourgeois upbringing" (114).

The main scapegoat character besides Zaza is, however, Simone
de Beauvoir's cousin Jacques. A gifted, even brilliant, adolescent, and
an enthusiastic young man, he introduced Simone de Beauvoir to a
great range of intellectual and artistic experiences—books, films, exhi-
bitions, plays—which were new to her: "I was dazed by all the new
things he revealed to me, so much so that I almost had the feeling
that he was the author of them all" (Memoirs, 202). But he is also
unstable, capricious, erratic, incapable of hard work, and, finally,
"very middle class" (Memoirs, 216), according to Simone. Her opinion of him alternates between admiration and condemnation. At
times she feels infatuated with him: "I was now certain that Jacques
thought a great deal of me, that he wanted me, and that I could live
with him in complete happiness" (Memoirs, 268); ultimately, though,
she rejects him because he does not resemble her idealized picture of
him: "this image of him in my mind" (293). She ends up by calling
him "a calculating bourgeois" (Memoirs, 347) when he contracts a
marriage of convenience. Finally, however, it is Jacques who becomes
an outcast, a tramp, an alcoholic, a "physical wreck . . . [dying] at
the age of forty-six of malnutrition" (Memoirs, 348). Unable to live up
to the ideal of the "great bourgeois gentleman" (349) which family

expectations had instilled in him but which did not agree with his taste and talents for art and literature, he was yet incapable of choosing the way out, away from those stifling expectations, except through self-destruction. Beauvoir invokes about him the same scapegoat myth she first mentions in connection with Zaza: "I believed he was more artistic, more sensitive, more spontaneous, and more gifted than myself; at times I would recall the story of Theagenus and Euphorion and I was prepared to set on a pedestal high above my own humbler qualities the special grace with which he seemed imbued" (*Memoirs*, 217). In many ways similar to Simone, and related to her by blood, Jacques had a fatal indolence, and his lack of strength and of willpower brand him as one of the scapegoats who buy her escape. By definition the surrogate victim does not get away, but makes it possible for the other—who might have been the victim—to do so.

Both Zaza and Jacques are at first seen as somehow "better" than Simone, and certainly as superior to the average run of girls and boys. More gifted, more sensitive, physically more handsome, they are truly exceptional children. From childhood on they bear also the stigmata of exceptional suffering. Zaza is marked by the severe burn-scars of a childhood accident on her flesh (*Memoirs*, 91); Jacques, whose father has died when he was two and whose mother seems to have more or less abandoned him after a second marriage, resembles a "little lord, dethroned, exiled, abandoned" (199). It is their unordinariness which separates them from the herd and makes them "sacrificeable" to use René Girard's expression ([1971] 1977, 270). Exceptional and exceptionally wounded they are natural brunt-bearers, and are easily destroyed as scapegoats.

The Scapegoat myth, like the Giant tale, is a self-justifying myth. It incorporates the shedding of people and milieus which marks Simone de Beauvoir's progress, and renders that shedding unavoidable, since, as a myth, it says: there must be scapegoats, some beings *are* scapegoats, and they redeem others.

The third mythic tale we read in the *Memoirs* is that of the Quester. Clues to the significant presence of this tale are given in the frequent allusions to the book *Le Grand Meaulnes* by Alain-Fournier. There are more references to this particular book and its author than to any other in the *Memoirs*.

When Henri Fournier (pen name: Alain-Fournier), aged twenty-eight, died in the World War I Battle of the Marne (September 1914) he left behind him some poems, a number of short stories, fragments of a novel and of a play, a vast correspondence, and, most importantly, one completed novel, published in 1913: *Le Grand Meaulnes* (translated into English as *The Lost Domain* and *The Wanderer.*) The success of this work has been enormous: it has been translated into thirty-three languages, studied in numerous theses, articles, and books, and turned into a ballet, a radio play and a film (Gibson 1975, 283); Robert Gibson declared in 1975 that "*Le Grand Meaulnes* is now safely established as a classic" (295). In 1979, however, Mechtild Cranston reported that "Alain-Fournier's name [was] omitted from two recent collective studies of the French novel," and asked: "Are the author's footprints lost among those of Zola and Proust, the giants of his age?" (1979, 377). Yet articles keep appearing and the book remains on the shelves of libraries and bookstores.

The novel tells the story of two adolescents, François Seurel, the narrator, and Augustin Meaulnes, schoolmates in a remote village of the deserted Sologne. In the course of an adventurous escapade in the desolate countryside, Meaulnes, nicknamed "Big Meaulnes," loses his way and stumbles on a mysterious manor house. A strange, magical, pleasure party is taking place there, attended by charmingly dressed children and kindly old people, and presided over by a young, beautiful, gentle girl, who seems to Meaulnes to embody "the most peaceful happiness on earth" (Alain-Fournier [1928] 1958, 60). After leaving the enchanted domain, Meaulnes is unable to find his way back to it, yet keeps yearning and searching for the old manor and for "the girl from the Lost land" ([1928] 1958, 132), signs of innocence, of childhood, of serene and perfect joy. When, after years of disillusionment and defilement, Meaulnes does seem to recover the lost past, this recovery is necessarily incomplete, flawed, and finally heartbreaking. The book is steeped in nostalgia, in the profound desire to return to a childhood state of grace, and in the particular oneiric atmosphere of adolescent phantasies and torments. Surely one of the reasons *Le Grand Meaulnes* has, over so many years, touched so many readers lies in the obvious mythic qualities that are deeply embedded in the book's structure and theme. The notion of a guiltless paradise, which, lost, becomes the object of a perilous quest, starts with the garden of Eden. The age of innocence, the golden age, Yeats' "woven world-forgotten isle," Baudelaire's "green paradise of childish loves," all vanish in life's upheavals, and innocence is transformed into a despairing and painful longing. The enigmatic aura, suggesting great significance, which envelops many of the novel's events, places, and characters, and the numerous fairy-tale motifs evident in many episodes (Cancalon 1975), all contribute to the mythic ambiance. Daniel Grojnowski says, correctly, that "*Le Grand Meaulnes* should be read as the description of a mythic universe, the projection of an interior landscape" (1964, 721).

Simone de Beauvoir tells in the *Memoirs* how she read the book "with tears in my eyes" (186), and names Meaulnes, the title character and hero of the work, among a list of fictional characters she particularly admired and wished to emulate: "I loved [them] . . . I would follow in their footsteps" (196). When she is fascinated by her cousin Jacques, she compares him to Meaulnes as "the perfect incarnation of Disquiet" (*Memoirs*, 201), and when he disappoints her, she confesses: "I had been badly mistaken in thinking he was a sort of Grand Meaulnes" (234). She lends the novel to Zaza, who reads it "three times over" (*Memoirs*, 221), and discusses it at length with her and other friends. As a presence in the *Memoirs*, Alain-Fournier's novel not only informs us about the reading preferences of Beauvoir and her friends but, more importantly, acts as a sign of yet another subterranean process of mythification at work. While the two previous tales—the Giant and the Scapegoat—are self-justifying myths, validating the young Simone's steady rise towards personal and intellectual self-affirmation accompanied by the progressive disappearance of cumbersome childhood bonds, this myth seems to go in the other direction: that of a desire to recapture childhood and its innocence. This quest would lead, not to supremacy, but to a regression into submission and littleness. While, obviously, this is not Simone de Beauvoir's overt intention, the myth signals and signifies a certain ambivalence toward her process of emancipation while at the same time softening what may seem to be the exaggerated harshness and resolution of her ambitions. It does thus play a double role—first in giving voice to a nostalgia for childhood and second in mitigating the ruthlessness with which Simone seems to have left childhood behind. In her article, "The Dream of Love: A Study of Three Autobiographies," Elaine Marks applies the term "quest" to what I call Beauvoir's "supremacy drive," and notes that "Simone de Beauvoir does not present childhood as a lost paradise. It is instead a necessary road that leads to freedom and implies a future" (1975, 80). That is, of course, correct, yet a nostalgic quest for childhood—overtly rejected, but covertly murmuring its claim—is present in the mythic underground of the *Memoirs*.

As in *Le Grand Meaulnes,* an "enchanted domain" has played a
great role in Simone's childhood: Meyrignac, the estate her grand-
father had inherited in the province of Limousin. There, and at La
Grillière, her uncle's estate, in the peaceful and unspoiled countryside, Simone and her family would spend a few blissful weeks each
summer. "My happiness used to reach its height during the two and
a half months which I spent every summer in the country" (*Memoirs,*
75) she writes, and "I could not imagine a more agreeable place to
live" (79). In the *Memoirs,* she recalls with evident pleasure the sensa-
tions of Meyrignac: "I let my ear be beguiled by the sounds of summer: the fizzing of wasps, the chattering of guinea-fowls, the
peacocks' strangulated cry, the whispering of leaves; the scent of
phlox mingled with the aromas of caramel and coffee and choco-
late that came wafting over to me from the kitchen; rings of sunlight
would be dancing over my exercise book. I felt I was one with
everything: we all had our place just here, now, and forever"
(*Memoirs,* 80).

That notion of having an enduring, durable place, of being in
place, of belonging in a place, which is one of the most seductive—
and smug—charms of the bourgeois life, is one Beauvoir will reject
eventually, of course, but as a child she is very sensitive to the entice-
ments of the perfect place, the summer place. There she could walk
with her sister, and explore the country: "We made great discoveries:
ponds; a waterfall . . . As we rambled along, we would sample the
hazelnuts and brambleberries in the hedges . . . We had bites out of
apples from every orchard . . . Drowsy with the scent of freshly
mown hay, with the fragrance of honeysuckle and the smell of buck-
wheat in flower, we would lie down on the warm moss or the grass
and read" (*Memoirs,* 80). Some of the most poetic, most beautifully
written, most touching passages in the *Memoirs* evoke Simone's summer memories of Meyrignac. There, as a child, she was at one with
the earth, and, through the presence of the earth, felt the living presence of God:

> I would rise in the middle of the night to look out upon the night
> breathing softly in its sleep. I would lean out and plunge my
> hands in the fresh leaves of a clump of cherry laurels; the water
> from the spring would be gurgling over a mossy stone; from
> time to time a cow would kick her hoof against the door of the

byre: I could almost smell the odour of straw and hay. Monotonous and dogged as the beat of the heart would sound the stridulations of a grasshopper; against the infinite silence and the sky's infinities I used to feel that the earth itself was echoing that voice within me which kept on whispering: "Here I am." My heart oscillated between its living warmth and the frigid blazing of the stars. There was God up there, and He was watching me." (*Memoirs*, 81–82).

But just as she discards God, so she detaches herself from Meyrignac: "I had wept at the thought that one day I would no longer feel at home at Meyrignac; that day had come . . . very soon, no doubt, I would never return there: but I didn't heave a single sigh of regret. My childhood and adolescence and the sound of the cows' hooves kicking the stable door as I leaned out into the starlit night—all that was far, very far behind me. Now I was ready for something else; I was all expectancy, and in the violence of this feeling all regrets were swept away" (*Memoirs*, 320). Even in this formulation of willful abandonment, however, nostalgia is present in the now distant echo of long-forgotten but profoundly remembered sounds.

To the world of Meyrignac, the world of childhood, belong also the unconditional and admiring love Simone had vowed her parents and family, and all the innocent occupations, amusements, and joys of a middle-class childhood—the carefully supervised schooling, the sweet piety of a religious education, family visits and other outings and treats—as well as the less innocent and carefully instilled awareness of being special by virtue of belonging to a certain class and to a certain family: "I belonged to an elite" (*Memoirs*, 47). That awareness, however, which on the social and political plane Simone will come to reject with all the other pretensions of her class, does not disappear totally; she incorporates it in her supremacy drive in which the notion of moral and intellectual superiority plays a large part.

While feelings of guilt are built into the Giant and the Scapegoat myths, at the same time that the exorcism of these feelings is also contained in both these mythic structures, guilt is even more, and more poignantly, present in the Quester's myth; Simone de Beauvoir's subconscious seems to beg all the abandoned people and places, all the rejected times and pleasures for forgiveness, by donning the identity of Meaulnes, the quester-for-childhood, who tries—in vain—to recapture the magic of his childhood adventure.

Beauvoir's quest for the past through the mythic tale redeems, at least in part, her ferocious drive to liberate herself from that past; her feeling of exile redeems the feeling of relief that exile causes. Her mythic regression allows her real progression, and serves as a palliative to its unstoppable momentum.

Georges Gusdorf remarks that "there is . . . a considerable gap between the avowed plan of autobiography, which is simply to retrace the history of a life, and its deepest intentions, which are directed toward a kind of apologetics or theodicy of the individual being" (1980, 39). The three mythic tales which we have examined play this role of apologetics, of theodicy or rather of autodicy: a vindication of the justice and rightness of the author's actions and desires. Our identification of these tales in the book does not radically alter Simone de Beauvoir's own overt presentation of her self-development. These tales do not run counter to that steady development; rather they reinforce the power of its drive by conferring upon it an almost compulsive necessity. At the same time, they allow the expression of hesitations and anxieties, making Beauvoir's self-development if anything more valuable, more heroic, because it is seen as having been acquired at great cost.

The Scapegoat and the Quester tales serve the myth of the Giant. While the Giant strides, the Scapegoat is sacrificed so that the Giant may continue her liberating progress, and the Quester, all the while, pursues a painful and redemptive pilgrimage. The Giant's project of conquest is the most important one, and it is supported on one side by the sacrifice of the victims who are doomed to destruction, and on the other by the torment of the suffering self. Thus the Giant's tale occupies the central place in the threefold mythic structure which, in its interwoven totality, constitutes the substructure, the wiring over which the first volume of Simone de Beauvoir's autobiography is able to stretch its visible shape, to extend its linear, vertical narrative of progress and ascent.

The *Memoirs* are the story of Beauvoir's access to the Book as a realm not only of free reading but of free writing, a realm in which she will spend the rest of her life, up to her death. In an interview with Francis Jeanson in 1966, when she was fifty-eight years old, she says that she does not consider her life an "enterprise" anymore, in the sense that, essentially, there will be no changes in it anymore, that her life will continue to be what it has been. "But," she says, "on the other hand, the enterprise of writing, yes, that is still real. To invent something each time, to create something new . . . I don't know very well anymore why I still feel that longing; but I *know* that I still feel it, and it is that what makes life, in a sense, also still an enterprise for me, insofar as my life consists also in the enterprise of writing" (Jeanson 1966, 192). The primacy accorded to the Book is evident in these words. Writing is living, and more than mere living. The Book has given her a voice, an impact, an enduring and fertile contact with the world she so wanted to dominate and possess. The triple mythic presence ultimately has the effect of lifting the story of Simone de Beauvoir's access to the Book from the level of the banal rebellion of one privileged girl against her milieu to a more exalted and exemplary plane, where a life becomes a destiny through the presence of passionate urgency and demanding, irrefutable need.

Notes

1. For a list of Simone de Beauvoir's writings up to 1978, including prefaces, interviews, and previously unpublished texts, see Claude Francis and Fernande Gontier, *Les écrits de Simone de Beauvoir.* See also Mary Evans' 1985 bibliography in *Simone de Beauvoir: A Feminist Mandarin.*

2. These titles are translated respectively as *Memoirs of a Dutiful Daughter, The Prime of Life, Force of Circumstance,* and *All Said and Done.*

3. In an article on Simone de Beauvoir's travels in and travel-writing about the United States, Mary McCarthy ironically calls her "Mlle Gulliver," and adds that "she has a child's greedy possessiveness toward this place [the United States] which she is in the act of discovering" (1976, 30).

4. The death of Zaza and Simone de Beauvoir's interpretation of it in the *Memoirs,* namely that Zaza dies so she, Simone, might go free, upsets many readers. So, for instance, Carol Ascher, who calls the last lines of the book "profoundly disturbing," and suggests that "perhaps Simone failed Zaza in some way" (1981, 187). Among a group of women to whom I presented an outline of this chapter, several were shocked by the "scapegoat" reading and its implications of ruthlessness on the part of Simone de Beauvoir. It remains, even in this last quarter of the twentieth century, a fact and an indication of women's still problematic access to the Book that while pursuing that access they must often seem ruthless, and must then be condemned for being so. The preference for "nice"—that is, nonaggressive, nonruthless—women remains, understandably enough, a cultural constant, while circumstances continue to reward the "masculine" virtues of aggression and strong drive toward a desired goal.

Simone de Beauvoir: Translated Works Cited

Memoirs of a Dutiful Daughter. (1958). 1974. Trans. James Kirkup. New York: Harper Colophon.
The Prime of Life. (1960). 1962. Trans. Peter Green. Cleveland: World Publishing Company.

For books and articles on Simone de Beauvoir, see the bibliographies in Whitmarsh 1981, Keefe 1983, and Evans 1985.

Works Cited

Alain-Fournier. (1928) 1958. *The Wanderer.* Trans. Françoise Delisle. New York: Limited Editions Club.
Ascher, Carol. 1981. *Simone de Beauvoir: A Life of Freedom.* Boston: Beacon Press.
Audet, Jean-Raymond. 1979. *Simone de Beauvoir face à la mort.* Lausanne: L'Age d'Homme.
Auerbach, Erich. (1946). 1957. *Mimesis.* Trans. Willard Trask. New York: Doubleday.
Bieber, Konrad. 1979. *Simone de Beauvoir.* Boston: Twayne.
Bruss, Elizabeth W. 1976. *Autobiographical Acts: The Changing Situation of a Literary Genre.* Baltimore: Johns Hopkins University Press.
Cancalon, Elaine D. 1975. *Fairy-Tale Structures and Motifs in le Grand Meaulnes.* Bern: Herbert Lang.
Cayron, Claire. 1973. *La nature chez Simone de Beauvoir.* Paris: Gallimard.
Cliche, Elène. 1984. "Simone de Beauvoir: l'incessante conquête." *Simone de Beauvoir Studies* 2: 24:41.
Cottrell, Robert D. 1975. *Simone de Beauvoir.* New York: Frederick Ungar.
Cranston, Mechtild. 1979. " 'La Marquise sort à cinq heures . . .' Symbol and Structure in Alain-Fournier's *Le Grand Meaulnes.*" *Kentucky Romance Quarterly* 26: 377–95.
Evans, Mary. 1985. *Simone de Beauvoir: A Feminist Mandarin.* London: Tavistock.
Francis, Claude, and Fernande Gontier. 1979. *Les écrits de Simone de Beauvoir.* Paris: Gallimard.

Gennari, Geneviève. 1958. *Simone de Beauvoir*. Paris: Editions Universitaires.

Gibson, Robert. 1975. *The Land Without a Name: Alain-Fournier and His World*. London: Paul Elek.

Gilligan, Carol. 1982. *In a Different Voice*. Cambridge: Harvard University Press.

Girard, René. (1971) 1977. *Violence and the Sacred*. Trans. Patrick Gregory. Baltimore: Johns Hopkins University Press.

_____. 1982. *Le Bouc Emissaire*. Paris: Grasset.

Grojnowski, Daniel. 1964. "Le Thème de la route dans l'oeuvre d'Alain-Fournier." *Critique* 208: 716–29.

Guiomar, Michel. 1964. *Inconscient et Imaginaire dans Le Grand Meaulnes*. Paris: Corti.

Gusdorf, Georges. 1980. "Conditions and Limits of Autobiography." Trans. James Olney. In *Autobiography: Essays Theoretical and Critical*. Ed. James Olney, 24–48. Princeton: Princeton University Press.

Hatcher, Donald L. 1984. *Understanding the Second Sex*. New York: P. Lang.

Hourdin, Georges. 1962. *Simone de Beauvoir et la Liberté*. Paris: Editions du Cerf.

Husson, Claudie. 1985. "Adolescence et création littéraire chez Alain-Fournier." *Revue d'Histoire Littéraire de la France* 85: 637–66.

Janeway, Elizabeth. 1980. "Women and the Uses of Power." In *The Future of Difference*. Ed. Hester Eisenstein and Alice Jardine, 327–44. Boston: G. K. Hall.

Jeanson, Francis. 1966. *Simone de Beauvoir ou l'entreprise de vivre*. Paris: Editions du Seuil.

Julienne-Caffié, Serge. 1966. *Simone de Beauvoir*. Paris: Gallimard.

Keefe, Terry. 1983. *Simone de Beauvoir: A Study of her Writings*. Totowa, N.J.: Barnes and Noble.

Lasocki, Anne-Marie. 1971. *Simone de Beauvoir ou l'entreprise d'écrire*. The Hague: Martinus Nijhoff.

Lejeune, Philippe. 1971. *L'Autobiographie en France*. Paris: Armand Colin.

_____. 1975. *Le Pacte autobiographique*. Paris: Editions du Seuil.

McCarthy, Mary. 1976. "Mlle Gulliver en Amérique." In *On the Contrary*, 24–31. New York: Octagon Books.

MacKeefe, Deborah. 1983. "Zaza Mabille: Mission and Motive in Simone de Beauvoir's *Mémoires*." *Contemporary Literature* 24: 204–21.

Madsen, Axel. 1977. *Hearts and Minds: The Common Journey of Simone de Beauvoir and Jean-Paul Sartre*. New York: William Morrow.

Marks, Elaine. 1973. *Simone de Beauvoir: Encounters with Death*. Brunswick, N.J.: Rutgers University Press.

———. 1975. "The Dream of Love: A Study of Three Autobiographies." In *Twentieth Century French Fiction: Essays for Germaine Brée*. Ed. George Stambolian, 72–88. New Brunswick, N.J.: Rutgers University Press.

Mehlman, Jeffrey. 1974. *A Structural Study of Autobiography*. Ithaca: Cornell University Press.

Olney, James. 1972. *Metaphors of Self: The Meaning of Autobiography*. Princeton: Princeton University Press.

———. 1980. "The Ontology of Autobiography." In *Autobiography: Essays Theoretical and Critical*. Ed. James Olney, 236–67. Princeton: Princeton University Press.

Renza, Louis A. 1980. "The Veto of the Imagination: A Theory of Autobiography." In *Autobiography: Essays Theoretical and Critical*. Ed. James Olney, 268–95. Princeton: Princeton University Press.

Simone de Beauvoir: Witness to a Century. Ed. Hélène Vivienne Wenzel. Yale French Studies 72 (1986).

Weintraub, Karl Joachim. 1978. *The Value of the Individual: Self and Circumstance in Autobiography*. Chicago: Chicago University Press.

Weitz, Margaret Collins. 1985. *Femmes: Recent Writings on French Women*. Boston: G. K. Hall.

Whitmarsh, Anne. 1981. *Simone de Beauvoir and the Limits of Commitment*. Cambridge: Cambridge University Press.

Hélène Cixous. Reprinted with kind permission of Hélène Cixous.

❧ 5 ❦

ℋélène Cixous

The Pervasive Myth

> Myths stubbornly pervade the way we treat one
> another and organize the space around us; they
> charge our works of art with urgent meaning.
>
> Albert Cook

> It is in writing, from woman and toward woman,
> and in accepting the challenge of the discourse
> controlled by the phallus, that woman will affirm
> woman somewhere other than in silence.
>
> Hélène Cixous

Hélène Cixous (b. 1937), one of the most widely known and
controversial French women writers today, is a professor of literature
at the University of Paris VIII-Vincennes (now situated at St. Denis),
which she co-founded in 1968 and where in 1975 she initiated the
Women's Studies Program. Already, before that date, her writings
were concentrating increasingly on problems of sexual difference and
of female writing and experience. On these subjects she has
written—and continues to write—a substantial number of critical-
theoretical texts, and what Ann Rosalind Jones calls "a growing collection of demonstrations of what id-liberated female discourse might
be" (1985, 365).[1] The latter, sometimes though wrongly described as
novels, are properly speaking "fictions"—works of an overwhelming
imaginative energy, in which "*tableaux*, poems, fables, images inter-
mingle endlessly" (Micha 1977, 115).

In both Cixous's theoretical and her fictional writings, myth
plays a prominent role. Indeed, to read, to study, to encounter Cixous's works is to plunge entirely into the world and the language of
myth, or rather of a wide spectrum of myths. Hers is, to use Pindar's
expression, a "many-mythed" universe (Cook 1980, 108) in which
mythologies such as the Egyptian and the Greek mingle and are
rewritten, and where female mythic figures of all kinds appear in
stately processions, in triumphal progressions, or in terrifying heca-
tombs, speaking in exuberant or meditative rhythms, in plaintive or
consoling voices. Cixous herself declares:

> "I work a lot on the level of myths . . . In reality, myth was that
> which took the place of analysis in former times . . . It showed
> that there was the universe, but one knew that there was also
> something else. One knew that something stronger than the
> social existed. I am passionately interested in myths, because
> they are always (this is well known) outside the law, like the
> unconscious. Only afterwards there is the story, which signifies
> that there has been a clash between the in-law and the
> out-law . . . What happens? Interpretation, of course, because
> we do have myths and their interpretations. One never
> questions enough the traditions of interpretation of myth, and
> all myths have been referred to a masculine interpretation. If we
> women read them, we read them otherwise. That is why I often
> nourish my texts, in my own way, at those mythic sources"
> (Conley 1984b, 155–56).

The "law" mentioned by Cixous is the law of traditional and
traditionally phallocentric authority, the law of the conventional social order (in which women are suppressed) and of established masculine discourse (in which the feminine is silenced). Women have
been outlaws: the title of the polemic book Cixous wrote with Catherine Clément, *La Jeune Née*, is a play on words on *la Genêt*, in an
allusion to the French writer Jean Genêt, here feminized by the article
la, whose life and writings were those of an outlaw, and therefore
akin to those of a woman.[2] Of course, *La Jeune Née* also means *The
Newly Born Woman*, for woman may, and must, escape the deathtrap
of the law—that is, of the arbitrary phallocentric order with all its
manifestations and implications, and give birth to her new freed self.

She may subvert the "old" order by stealing into it, as it were, through a reappropriation, a stealing back, of the myths that had been stolen from her in the first place. A total reinterpretation of the myths that are part and parcel of Western culture would shake the conceptual foundations of that culture, of that dead order. Cixous formulates here a project also proposed by Mary Daly, namely a reading *otherwise* of myths: "Women can discover and create our myths in the process of a-mazing tales that are phallic" (Daly 1978, 47). The use of myths (transformed, remade, inverted) is therefore the keystone of a methodology of female self-discovery and self-expression, of rebirth, recovery, rewriting. This subversive use of myth allows the expression in language of "whatever it is that lies beneath or beyond language" (Cook 1980, 266): for Cixous, the hitherto "invisible, foreign, secret, hidden, mysterious, black, forbidden" (*Newly Born* 1986, 69) domain of women.

Hélène Cixous herself seems to be a quasi-mythic figure as she is described by Verena Andermatt Conley:

At the former Vincennes, in a school notorious for a certain regal squalor—windows fissured, chairs piled helter-skelter in corners, posters stapled in magnificent collages of spectral filth over walls and windows, serving as milieu for an outstanding faculty of generally left-wing thinkers—Cixous used to enter the complex in a dazzling ermine coat whose capital worth most probably surpassed the means of many in the classroom. Her proxemics marked a progressive use of repression. As a replica of Bataille's evocation of Aztec ceremony, she surged from the context of the cheaply reinforced concrete of classroom shelters. She then became a surplus value and a zero-degree term, the sovereign center of a decorous, eminently caressive body where her politics splintered those of an archaic scene in which the king would have his wives circulate about him. Because of the rite of such a scene, which leads to writing on the part of all participants, Cixous's subjects celebrate her gift of energy. . . . At the beginning of every seminar she unbuckles her belt: a half-cuirass. Her strap frees the body and disintegrates the militant civic order of the practical world; this is indeed a sensuous militancy that calls her audience to write both with and against the male, to write when the strap undoes the pressures needed to protect and chastize the uterus in the male order. Such are the lures of a modern Cleopatra, a magnanimous neo-Natura who forces the woman in writing to unbuckle the clothing with which she has had to be preserved (Conley 1984, 80–81).

What are we to make of this remarkable description? It certainly demonstrates most effectively Cixous's personal mythic-didactic impact on those who approach her, and, in Conley's case, write about her. Conley's is the only book so far written about Cixous, and where other scholars have produced papers on Cixous, or included her in studies of a larger scope, Conley has written a truly Cixous-ian book, in which she adopts Cixous's style, her mythic-poetic language, and her rhythms in order to convey, to approach, the reality of Cixous's being and writing. In Conley's description, the mythic Cixous is seen as the goddess and the priestess of her own rites ("writes"). The Aztec ceremony described by Bataille is one of human sacrifice, in which "a slave-girl, representing the goddess Ilamatecultli . . . entirely dressed in white" (Bataille 1976, 57) was killed in a temple named Coatlan. Cixous subverts that archaic rite of immolation. Her ceremonial use of the squalid transgressive spaces of the experimental Paris VIII-Vincennes classrooms destroys the Coatlan tradition of sacred spaces dedicated to ritual death. Repression is re-enacted and thereby transformed into liberation. This liberation, performed by Cixous through the unbuckling of her confining leather belt, is a preliminary rite to that of giving birth, giving writing. The woman in writing is the woman who is pregnant with text, ready to give birth to it and thus to herself, and Cixous is both the teacher-seducer who has impregnated her subjects with the necessary energy, the force of life, and the teacher-midwife who assists at the birth. She herself testifies to this process when she says that woman "must revive herself, recover her vital forces, she must dare *herself*, she must dare to be herself. I have verified this with my female students in a most astounding manner; in two years I have seen women of all ages being born" (Makward 1976, 26). The mythic weight of Cixous's ritual performance, which so transforms the ordinary classroom experience as to make it unrecognizable, is analogous to the mythic impact of her writings, which are very consciously "different." Just as the reinterpretation of myths may restore woman to herself and to her own truth, so may the remaking of the act of writing, conjointly and simultaneously, reinstate woman in the realm of the Book, where her truth may be expressed.

For Hélène Cixous, the Book becomes *écriture féminine*—feminine writing. The expression, which, Cixous admits, is "a dangerous and stylish expression full of traps, which leads to all kind of confusions" (Conley 1984b, 129), is now widely used to evoke a much-debated critical and theoretical notion.[3] Grounded in Cixous's readings of Derrida and Freud/Lacan, and intended to extend or critique these readings, it is a notion which lifts the act of writing out of the phallocentric, patriarchal domain where Western culture has situated it, in order to de-place it and to re-place it in the libidinal-maternal realm of *féminité*, a realm of desire, of passion, of love, where the experience of the body is valorized and linked with the experience of language. While this realm is not reserved for women, they do have "a privileged access to it" (Jardine 1985, 262),[4] as they also have the greatest need of it. Indeed, for women, *écriture féminine* may be used, as Sandra Gilbert says, as "a fundamentally political strategy, designed to redress the wrongs of culture through a revalidation of the rights of nature" (1986, xv). Nature, life, giving birth, mothering, female giving, as well as the female unconscious and female pleasure, all are concepts that have been either repressed or hideously perverted and pressed into the service of the patriarchal construct. Cixous restores to these concepts their rightful autonomy and original, free, life-affirming power. They are the informing notions of the truly female text, which is a text of life: "For Cixous . . . the act of speaking and, even more, of writing as a female represents a fundamental birth drive which will destroy the old order of death, not merely its material, economic, social, and political manifestations, but the generative system, which determines the production of meaning" (Stanton 1980, 78).

In her essay, "The Laugh of the Medusa" (published in French in 1975 and in English in 1976), Hélène Cixous issued a very influential, inspired, fiery manifesto of women's writing, asking women "Why don't you write? Write! Writing is for you, you are for you; your body is yours, take it" (876), and telling them to write with "white ink" (881), that is, the mother's milk with which women may nourish each other. All of Cixous's work since then has been concerned with women's coming to writing. She refuses to define a feminine practice of writing, for to do so would be to enclose it in a theory, a code, a static and eventually stagnant system, while it should be a perpetually ongoing dynamic process, a movement, a breaking of boundaries, a challenging of authority, an inventing of new representations of hitherto suppressed realities. For the same reason she refuses to produce theory, in spite of her evident contribution to feminist thought, because the traditional discourse of theory is seen by her as confining and overly rigorous. The unbuckling of her corset-belt in class likewise signifies her refusal to adopt a specific discourse. She acknowledges her debts to Heidegger, Derrida, and other philosophers, but refuses to bend her thinking to the structures of theirs, her writing to the rules of philosophical discourse. Her example here is the poet Rilke; he, she says, "did not have to produce theory. Heidegger did that for him. Rilke, with the peculiar instrument infinitely freer than philosophical discourse, produced a series of works that are living objects in which you see, for example, how a rose opens up. In a certain way, poetry is disenfranchised from the obligation that philosophy has: to demonstrate, justify" (Conley 1984, 152).

Like Rilke, Cixous does not have to produce theory. She chooses instead the path of mythic-poetic expression for her "theoretical" and her imaginative writings. Poetry is able to give voice to that which is silenced in rational, logical discourse. In the words of Audre Lorde: "For women, then, poetry is not a luxury. It is a vital necessity of our existence. It forms the quality of the light within which we predicate our hopes and dreams toward survival and change, first made into language, then into idea, then into more tangible action. Poetry is the way we help give name to the nameless so it can be thought. The farthest external horizons of our hopes and fears are cobbled by our poems, carved from the rock experiences of our daily lives" (1980, 126).

Analogous to poetry in its powers, myth is able to name the figures who oppose the discourse of suppression, or have been victimized by it, and to propose them as paradigms—reread and renewed—of female experience. In the wake of Cixous's defiantly laughing Medusa follow Medea, Ariadne, Antiope, Hippolyta, the Amazons, Phaedra, Electra, Penthesileia, Promethea, Dido, Cleopatra, and countless others, named, nameless, or endowed with names by Cixous. For her all women, because of their long confinement in silence and darkness, partake of the qualities of the mythic: mystery and a certain aura of eternity, of antiquity, of always-having-been, even when occulted by society: "So it is with people who exist so strongly so mysteriously: (women especially) when you meet them for the first time you feel you have known them for such a long time. . . . You never know when you see them coming absentmindedly down the stairs if these women are coming from their room or from antiquity" (Cixous 1984, 39).

While Cixous refers to authors such as Kleist, Hoffman, Rilke, or Blanchot as to familiars, writers who "let their femininity traverse them" (Conley 1984b, 152), the writer who is, so to speak, her "soul mate" (Armbruster 152), in whom myth and poetry combine most perfectly, is the Brazilian author Clarice Lispector (1925–77). Cixous's article "L'Approche de Clarice Lispector" is a hymn to the magic powers of Clarice: powers of being, of waiting, of seeing, of voicing, of giving, or revealing. Cixous sings a mythification of the dead Lispector as a woman already come to writing, in full possession of her reality, and lovingly, passionately willing to guide other women to the same discoveries she has made, to teach them the crucial approaches. Clarice Lispector is "Clarisque," the risk of confronting the horror of reality in order to gain its joy; she is "la voix-Clarice," both voice (*voix*) and road (*voie*) for women who hear her "appel clarice" (her claricean call); she is "l'écriture-une-femme," writing incarnated in woman. She is also "lispectorange": an allusion to Cixous's book *Vivre l'orange* (1979), for which "Clarice Lispector becomes Cixous's engendering source" (Conley 1984b, 105), and a play on "Oran-je" (Oran-I) since Cixous was born in Oran, Algeria. The neologism *lispectorange* unites the woman writer as birth giver, the place of birth, and the birthed I. *Lispectorange* also means Lispector-angel, alluding to the Brazilian writer's tutelary guardian powers. Lispector, in all the metamorphoses, or rather avatars, with which Cixous endows her in "L'Approche de Clarice Lispector" is a completely mythic figure: initiator, visionary, priestess of women's most urgent rite, their coming to the Book. Carol Armbruster is correct in remarking that "in contrast to narcissistic writing, which appropriates everything to its author-ized center, Lispector's writing is [for Cixous] an *écriture-fenêtre* (text-window) through which we pass into the immediate, uncodified life of the now-moment, and the other that it is, in all its sensuality and strangeness. Her writing receives the other in its living totality and attempts to relate its life and fullness through a language that calls and names it without possessing or dominating it, without transforming it in any way, and without denying its difference" (1983, 150–51).

The female conquest of the Book, exemplified by Clarice Lispector, is at the core, implicitly or explicitly, of most of Cixous's writings. It is particularly clear in her book *Illa* (1980)—"She, The One, That

One"—a myth of loss and absence transformed into reconquest and presence. *Illa* is written in Cixous's typical fluid, chanting, incantatory style which has been compared to James Joyce's stream-of-consciousness writing. Conley calls it "a supple, pre-Cartesian mold of language richer in associative range and far more cohesive in sensorial substance of flesh and word than fiction . . ." (1984, 54): that is, a poetic language. Cixous coins words and distorts words, plays with words and with syntax, with meanings and suggestions, with metaphors and allusions, alliterations and rhythms. Few French writers since Rabelais have taken the liberties with language she dares to take. For this she has been bitterly attacked. As Christiane Makward has pointed out, she has provoked "the most diverse reactions: rage, laughter, hatred, admiration, boredom (a polite variant on rage) and even a nobler one: anxiety!" (1978, 319). Of course she has been branded as illegible and thus as elitist. The truth is that all readers willing to make the effort to free themselves of preconceived notions of what "fiction" should be and contain, and to enter into the stream of Cixous's language, will be amply rewarded by the beauty and the magic of these eminently poetic texts, and by the mythic power radiating from them with a rare pervasive and revelatory force.

Cixous herself says about her texts that "what is important is the vocal element, the musical element, language at its most archaic and, at the same time, its most elaborate level" (Rossum-Guyon 1977, 488). Her texts are crowded with the most diverse intertextual and intercultural references, not all of which will be understood by all readers, but, as she remarks: "A text is like a city, like a museum: you walk around in it, and you perceive what appeals to you" (Rossum-Guyon 1977, 489), and the fact that all references are not deciphered by everybody is less important than the total communicative impact of the text's sounds, images, and luscious sensuality. Cixous's writings are to be accepted as myths and then read, not with the decoding, categorizing mind of the anthropologist, but with the hungry, thirsty mind of the original seeker of myths, that is, of answers which, in their shape and peculiar clarity, surpass the realm of logic. While such a reading may be a dizzying and disconcerting activity, it may also offer exhilaration, discovery, and understanding through the empowering contact with female myths.

Illa takes its title from Virgil's *Georgics:* "Illa: 'Quis et me' inquit 'miseram et te perdidit, o tu, quis tantus furor?' " ("She cried out, 'What wild fury ruins us, my pitiable self and you?' ") (4.494).[5] This line, quoted in the first paragraph of Cixous's text, is the expression of Eurydice's anguish when, for the second time, and now for good, she has to leave the world for the underworld, condemned by Orpheus's heedless act to death and darkness. Indeed, as Virgil continues the mythic tale and Eurydice's plaint we hear her bemoan her fate: "See, once again the cruel fates call me back/ And once more sleep seals closed my swimming eyes. Farewell: prodigious darkness bears me off" (4.495–97). While the Orphic song keeps ringing, Eurydice—*Illa*—remains encased in silence and in perpetual absence. But Cixous frees Illa, delivering her from the grip of nonbeing through her "infinite belief in transformations" (Conley 1984b, 15): she transforms Illa into Proserpina/Persephone/Kora, another mythic figure assigned to the realm of death, but rescued by the ceaseless search and the need of her mother, Ceres/Demeter.

By shifting from the Orphic myth to the Ceres-Proserpina tale, Cixous shifts from a story of death to one of life, of seeking life, of overcoming death by seeking. The first words of the book are: "Who? Am The third one. Runs at the edge of the earth, the sea. *Quis* [Who]? Am we? Who? I? We? Roams outside of herself. *Illa*. A young person. The third one" (1980a, 7).[6] Cixous posits here, through the repeated questions, the importance of the notion of seeking; she also posits here for the first time a notion that she will elaborate throughout the book: that of a female trinity, whose oneness is indicated by Cixous's grammatical twisting—transforming, again—of the language, so that the first person singular verb ("am") and the first person plural personal pronoun ("we") lock into each other and generate a new form: "we am." She defines this female trinity as consisting of "the first First and her daughter the second and the third, sometimes called Demeter and Persephone, often simply called 'the Goddesses' or the apples" (*Illa*, 203). The daughter is the lost one (the second) *and* the to-be-found and found one (the third). The "Third" is, then, also the being in whom mother and daughter are one (as in the Christian Trinity, God the Holy Ghost signifies the unity of the Father and the Son.) As "Goddesses" they (she + she + she) offer exemplary images of and for all women and as "apples" they signify the gifts women give each other.

The Christian Holy Trinity is defined as "three persons really distinct, equal and consubstantial, in one only and indivisible nature" (*Dictionnaire* 1968, 790), and the Holy Ghost as "that what (or he who) divinises us, and makes us participants in the divine nature, and gives us the Spirit of the Son, which permits us to say *Abba* to the Father" (*Dictionnaire* 1968, 271). Analogously, Cixous's Third one is distinct yet inseparable, in the consubstantial unity of female bodily and spiritual experience, from the First one (the Mother) and the Second one (the lost daughter) but it is she (the Third one) who makes the giving intercourse between the other two possible. It is Illa, the Third, whose name means "she" (i.e., everywoman), also called Illa-Ipsa: she herself, or she-the-same (i.e., the same in one nature as the First and the Second, and as all women) who is woman complete, tri-une, triumphant.

Her name is also "Ile à île" (*Illa*, 24): Island to island and "Et" (And). "An 'And' becomes real," writes Cixous, "and opens up each time a woman gives birth to one of her mothers. And each time a woman asks to receive light from another woman . . . A woman gives a heavy breath of life to a woman: and an And is" (*Illa*, 202). Illa/And is thus the incarnation of bridging (island to island), of conjunction, of life-giving connection between women who also give each other apples, roses, voices, texts, children. The Demeter-Persephone story is a mother-daughter story of seeking, saving, restoring life, and the model of female texts: "The story of the coming-and-going and the bringing-forth of a sister by her twin is the matrix of fiction" (*Illa*, 25). Mother, daughter, sister: all are identical twins and children/mothers of each other through their womanhood and through their reciprocal, continuous, birth-giving. For Cixous it is the only story: the story of what happens between women.

In the text of Claudian, *De Raptu Proserpinae*, translated by Catherine des Roches, the Ceres-Proserpina story is fragmented, cut short: Proserpina is only shown as lost. For Cixous she is, most importantly, the sought and found one. However, in the first part of *Illa* the accent is on Ceres/Demeter's loss, on the daughter's absence. Bitter questions and smarting cries resonate across the pages: "A mother without the maternal daughter?" (27). "A mother without a daughter—what is left?—a less-mother" (28). "A mother suddenly without answer. Unmade. She who made her, suddenly, taken away. A dis-invested mother. Breath [Cixous makes this grammatically masculine word feminine: *la* souffle, instead of *le*: breath = life = woman] cut off. Her daughter, the strength of her strength, the source of her sources, her truth incarnate, the triply beloved . . ." (*Illa*, 26). "I have lost my sight. My eyes look for her, do not find her" (41).

The ravished Persephone is "sous taire" (under silence) (*Illa*, 923), a typically Cixousian pun on "sous terre" (under the earth). She has been ravished while picking "un fleur blanc": Cixous masculinizes the feminine noun "fleur" (flower) and specifies that the white flower which led to Persephone's doom is a narcissus: male narcissism and narcissistic self-absorption (i.e., exclusion of the other) threaten woman as "the earth opens up and the li-uncle roars" (*Illa*, 14). The lord of the Underworld, Pluto, is Demeter's brother and therefore Persephone's incestuous uncle: a "li-uncle," akin to the lion; a dangerous, devouring creature; a wild beast of prey.

The *sous terre/sous taire* pun makes it clear that the Demeter-Persephone story is one about women's loss of and struggle for expression, for voice, for writing, for text. The Third is "une écriture. Kore" (a writing, Kora) (*Illa* 1980a, 10). Persephone/Proserpina is thus often called by her other name of Kora: "Bring into accord Kora to Cordelia—through Kor, through sympathy, through correspondences: the elements of this seeking story are seeking stories—and if this story is a story of writing [*écriture*], of a woman, addressing herself/itself in flesh and in chant [pun on "chant" = song, and "sang" = blood] to a she, seeking her, addressing her, and [if] that singing keeps close to the edge of the sea [pun again on "mer" = sea, and "mère" = mother] then she/it [i.e., the story, the woman] has at least three elements. Do you follow us?" (*Illa*, 12). Puns are a way for Cixous to make language yield all its possible hidden meanings, so that "meanings radiate, multiply, permeate the text" (Kuhn 1981, 40). The last words of the quote—"Do you follow us?"—are in French "Tu nous suis?" and may be translated as "You we am?" thus once again evoking the plurality, the trinity, and the unity contained in and existing between women. Translated as "Do you follow us?" the same words transform the docile following of Proserpina on Orpheus's footsteps (leading to her death) into a chain of women—including the reader, to whom the question is also addressed—following one another into life.

"Kor"—embodied and embedded in Cordelia and in Kora/Persephone/Proserpina—is both heart (*cor* in Latin) and body (*corps* in French). Significantly, Cixous writes *Kor* rather than *Cor*, as common Latin usage dictates, preferring the ancient letter *k* of the Latin alphabet to the newer *c* which eventually replaced it. Cixous advocates fidelity to sources, to origins. She values "the Egyptian language, whose words do not deny their origins, do not repress what they do not say" (*Illa*, 40), and woman, "whose roots are more ancient than those of reason" (40). *Kor* allied to *Kora* (with her Greek *kappa*) is the union of body and soul also inscribed in Cordelia. Verena A. Conley points out the multiple resonances of this name: "Cordélia is a *corps-délit*, a criminal body, the crime of having a body, a bodily idea. That which unbinds, *délie* . . . *Corps d'elle il y a*: a body of she there is, or *corde il y a*: there is a thread which links Koré to Cordelia, a thread that is cut between mother and daughter, between *elle* and *elle*, she and she. Also *corps-ai*, body I have, and cor = coeur, the heart, the seat of feeling or, in a Heideggerian sense, source and shelter" (Conley 1984b, 112). Cordelia is also, of course, Lear's rejected daughter— rejected for speaking with her own voice. Victim of a narcissistic and blind father, she becomes the daughter of a father transformed, by one of Shakespeare's painful and quasi-miraculous transformations, into a feminine male, a seeker and a giver, a being who, having been deprived of sight, may yet see (as women, having been deprived of voice, may yet speak.)[7]

Seeking and giving are key gestures in this mythic tale of *écriture féminine*, and they remind us of Catherine des Roches' Agnodice, seeking to help, dispensing life-saving help and consolation through the gift of nourishing female access to the Book, signified by her "twin apples." "Restore me with apples": this sentence from the *Song of Songs* is, for Cixous, "the sentence all women utter" (*Illa*, 88). Throughout *Illa*, apples signify giving between women, just as all of *Illa* is a gift, "an apple of a text."[8] As in the story of Agnodice, but in a much more pronounced way, the female body is the locus of writing. Giving birth = giving writing, and vice versa, not metaphorically, but literally, corporally; both bring forth body and soul: woman. A desire for giving and receiving life equals a desire for giving and receiving writing: "There is that pressure, deep down, at the extremity of the world, against the abdominal wall, . . . that need for expression, in the bottom of one's belly, that obstination, fight against immobility, that hand against the walls of absence . . . no other force but the essence of desire" (*Illa* 1980a, 25).

The malediction/interdiction against female writing is demonstrated through yet another myth—that of Leto, forbidden by Hera to give birth "in any spot where the least ray of sunlight shines" (*Illa* 1980a, 48). She is told: "You will not give birth. You will not bring a child into the world" (*Illa*, 47), an interdiction similar to the one pronounced against women who want to write, to "gain access to a promised language" (58), to give birth into "that language without fear which excells at not being silent" (40). Women's bodies and souls are deprived and frustrated together: where, how to give birth? Where, how to write? These are identical questions for Cixous. Leto joins Demeter, joins the masses of women seeking answers to these questions.

Writing calls women as does the child about to be born (or found, re-born): "A call from an alien land. Writing. A person writes. A person calls; writing has telephoned. A voice from very far away, from very close by; 'Come and get me! I am getting lost!' From closer than close: 'Call me back! Look for me! I am obliterated here!' Full of fear, the called one's only desire is to call back, but where? Here, here, closer by, still more immediately, more strangely close. The called one remains voiceless. Mute, she listens, cannot make another word. It is the ears now who work. Who seek the voice" (*Illa*, 57).

The image of the telephone, which occurs several times in the book, may seem incongruous, but the telephone line, it is clear, is also a sign of the life line, the connecting line, Ariadne's line into and out of the labyrinth. The telephone line is not different from the criss-cross lines made by the "ceaseless shuttles, the comings and goings, of the mother" (Demeter), travelling the earth "seeking to read the traces of her dear disappeared one" (*Illa* 1980a, 67). Making lines, spinning threads, establishing connections—through thought, voice, touch, any sort of reaching out—are all actions of seeking. Ariadne the line-giver and Arachne the web-spinner become one in Ariachne, the sign of weaving and spinning: of binding, conjoining woman. Spinning is not a deadening activity here, as it was for the Dames des Roches, but a self-seeking and self-affirming enterprise, as Mary Daly also interprets it: "In this space [i.e., the female space] she [i.e., woman] can begin to weave the tapestries of her own creation. With her increasing fire and force, she can begin to Spin. As she and her sisters Spin together, we create the network of our time/space" (1978, 320). In *Illa*, the tapestry Ariachne weaves is also a statement of violent denunciation, as she weaves into her work (like Philomela did!) an account of the male-inflicted sufferings undergone by such female mythic figures as Leda, Demeter, Kora, Ariadne, Medusa, and by "all women who did not find it charming to be bitten, torn, stabbed in the back, petted with rams' horns [or] with fangs of serpents, talons of eagles, hooves, beaks" (*Illa*, 71).

Who are these victimizers? Cixous calls them "the old perverse ones . . . the insect-like ones" (*Illa* 1980a, 71), embodied in the Ceres-Proserpina myth by Pluto, the ravisher. They are the destroyers of life and of female writing, the uncles ("oncles") who separate woman from her mother by a "coup d'oncle" that is, an "uncle-scratch," a pun on "coup d'ongle," a (nail) scratch. Their laws are the laws of the underworld, as they impose silence, absence, and death on women. These are the same laws against which Madeleine and Catherine de Roches had spoken four centuries earlier. They are the laws determining Eurydice's undoing, and Persephone's rape and abduction; the laws stifling all creativity, all breathing. But women may restore the pulsations of breath and life to each other, to all women: "A woman came to me from the edges of another life, she took me on her knees, she suckled me. If in me Cordelia breathes again after I expired on her lips, it is because a woman heard my silence in Cordelia and has breathed for me when I choked" (*Illa*, 83).

With these lines finishes the first part of the book. This part bears no title, but it might be called "Illa vanished," or "Illa imprisoned," or "Illa en-coffered" (as this is a frequent image of sequestration in the text), to parallel the title "Illa delivered," which heads the second part.

The first part echoes with themes and code-like words (for in the substance and density of words are comprised and as it were sensualized what would conventionally be called themes) which sound also through the two other parts. It is impossible, and would be foolish, to look for a logical, linear progression in this book which, like all of Cixous's fictions about women, is much more like a prose poem or a word-tapestry, a chant or a prolonged incantation, than like a novelistic narrative. If there is any discernible structure, it is that of a progression which, because of the constantly woven and interwoven, interlaced, texture of the book, always reintegrates the whole of the tale in its accretive unwinding. Nothing is discarded from the text. Like musical motifs, recurrent forms, shapes, and figures form an ever-widening design, based on repetition, variation, and ever-expanding amplification.

Of course there are no "characters" in the conventional sense. Talking about "The Character of 'Character' " Cixous has written about authors she admires—Georges Bataille, James Joyce, Hoffman, and Kleist—that they were "poets of Subversion, deposers of conservative narcissism, breakers of yokes and shackles," citing as proof of their liberating capacity for subversion their treatment of the "character": "They tear away the subject from subjugation, rip up personal possession, dismember the marionette, cut the strings, distort the mirrors. Early on Hoffman set free the complicated intoxication of knowing that 'I' is more than one" (1974, 389). In *Illa*, "I" and "we" blend with countless figures and are integrated into the female myth. Besides the emblematic shapes of Demeter and Persephone, transcended into Illa, there are others (not really other, but forms of the same) such as the Egyptian Isis, "the mother who returns" (*Illa*, 13); the Amazons; Cybele; Greta Garbo (whose flat sandals and searching stride recall Persephone's); Freud's much violated, manipulated, but resistant and rebellious Dora, gliding goldenly through the water-text as a "Daurade," a golden fish;[9] and especially Angela, the *alter ego* of Clarice Lispector. *Illa* is animated, as it were, by Lispector, whose image is the all-encompassing, the all-pervading one. "Angela" and the "Autor" are the voices and presences in Lispector's posthumously published *Um Sopro de Vida*, subtitled *Pulsações*.

"Pulsations"—the rhythms of blood and breath, of moving and palpitating life—are everywhere in *Illa*. On the last page of the book we read: "I hear already her pulsacoes" (*Illa* 1980a, 212), but already, in the first part, the mother-woman-seeker listens for "the rapid pulsations of the secret under the base of the silent regions" (57). When Demeter's daughter is forcibly brought to the underworld, "the weight of Sicily crushes her breast, Etna [from whose flowery slopes Persephone was abducted] weighs on her forehead and crushes her temples, stuffs her ears with lava, spits in her throat the ashes which bury all sounds as soon as they are born. But the mute one persists, does not die, remains between non-life and the way out, waits for the breathing to grow again" (*Illa*, 25). Angela-Clarice are eminently capable of restoring life and breath, of "giving back to the mother maternity . . . of repairing the absence . . . of translating love into our most foreign languages" (*Illa*, 82–83). As such, they are part of a chain of women who "do not meet, have never seen one another, but hear each other, feel each other, keep each other loved, across the winters, across the frozen earth" (*Illa*, 83).

The last section of the first part is entitled, "A typical difficulty: the choice of the subject" (*Illa* 1980a, 47), and, while it repeats all the themes from the preceding sections—the disappearance, the search, the importance of female connections—it also stresses that women should be on the alert to choose, in their searches, the right directions, to make the right decisions. Cixous uses here the metaphor of the test or exam women have to pass on that *dies illa dies irae* (the Third's name now implying a possibility of disaster, of the *ira*, the wrath, of the old ones crushing her, or alternatively, of women's ire finally finding voice) when it is important to give the right answers to the right questions. The old ones, the representatives of the oppressive, death-dealing, killing laws, are always ready to insinuate their ideas, their "grey" (i.e., insidious, almost imperceptible, but dangerously seductive) attractions into woman's mind and body, so that "finally she finds herself alienated, and, in spite of herself, is ready to let herself sink irresistibly in her own abyss, in which we [she = we] would succumb . . ." but then Cixous adds immediately, "if one or the other of our sixty women friends of the same age did not recall us to our true project: the choice a woman desires to make between two destinies." (*Illa*, 62).

"Illa delivered" is the second part of this loosely *and* tightly structured work. It is both, in the sense I have already indicated: there is no conventionally coherent and logical narrative structure, but, on the other hand, there is a pervasive and persuasive mythic coherence, and thus a continuous coincidence of motifs throughout the book. The unbroken fluidity of mythic-poetic interlace, which finally turns the book into one urgent, lyrical chant, is reinforced by the connections between the parts. The first word of the second part is "because," continuing the notion which preceded it at the end of part one: women may be saved "because a woman does not give in to death unless she has forgotten the secret of her strength" (*Illa*, 84).

This second part continues to explore the dangers for women and their indispensable solidarity, as mysterious but strong life lines tie them together. Less emphasis is placed on the loss of Proserpina here. That loss is recalled by allusions to Sicily—a code word for the Ceres-Proserpine myth—and to "the mother of the woman sought all over the world" (*Illa* 1980a, 88), and loss is always kept in mind as a possibility and a threat. The accent, however, is on women defying death and despair together, and giving each other life—loving each other. Women touch each other across distances, and, with "a galilean hand," give each other wisdom, apples, living things. The "galilean" hand of women implies Galileo's triumphant knowledge ("eppur si muove" quotes Cixous (*Illa* 1980a, 89]), but also Christ's—the Galilean's—power of redemption.[10] Angela and Clarice are increasingly the great presences here: glorious, undaunted incarnations of "she, the Third one, a writing" (*Illa*, 92). And there is Renate as well, "the re-birther, my tenacious friend" (110), who "ran to the edge of disparition, called me, held me back" (113), and "all our persistent women friends" (115), all the nameless, faceless women to whom other women owe debts of children, of writing, of knowledge, of truth. All these women give, give, give ceaselessly, and send each other on their way to writing.

In her essay "Castration or Decapitation?" Cixous had already explored the importance of the female gift: "the question a woman's text asks is the question of giving . . . you might say it 'gives a send-off' . . . [which is] really giving, making a *gift* of departure . . ." (1981, 53). In *Illa* the gift is, as we have seen, the central, necessary fact. Conley analyzes the problematics of the gift, as it was popularized and studied in France through the writings of Claude Lévi-Strauss and Marcel Mauss, and concludes that "for Cixous as well as for others, the gift as excess, as spending and abundance, becomes, because of her cultural position in (Western) society, woman's essential attribute; because she has always been repressed culturally, she is more capable of giving than man" (1984b, 18).[11]

The last line of the second part leads again directly into the third, last, part, entitled "Calm School of Approaches" (*Illa* 1980a, 134), which continues the exploration of loving and giving between women, the essence of female texts. While the same themes continue to be treated with playful, enriching, enchanting variations, the stress is now on what women need to do in order to enact their loving and giving into writing. They have to be able to wait, and they have to be able to embrace and be faithful to life, the world, the earth, the body, simple objects, natural things (an egg, a flower, a tree), not hectically, not frantically, but in the calm and confident, patient preparation of the essential readiness that precedes writing-birthing.[12] Woman has to penetrate, or repenetrate, since she knew it in childhood, into the garden of language/experience Cixous calls "the Garden of Essays" (*Illa*, 137): that is, the garden of attempts, of experiences/experiments ("essayer" = to try), of being (Latin "esse"), of eating (German "essen"); it is the Garden of "it is" ("des c'est," 139), of "the Hers" ("des Ses," 146), and "of And" ("de Et," 199).

This garden, the "where" women were looking for, replaces the punitive and exclusive garden of Eden with the fresh innocent garden world of women's newly discovered, newly born language, guaranteed by female connections, and by fidelity to the rich realities the earth offers to be smelled, tasted, heard, seen. Clarice is already there, and her name, magically multiplied, fills the air and illuminates the garden space with shimmering reflections: "Claricelispector. Clar. Ricelis. Celis. Lisp. Clasp. Clarisp. Clarilisp-cla-spec-tor-lis-icelis-isp-larice-rice-pector-clarispector-claror-listor-rire-clarice-respect-rispect-clarispect-ice-clarici. O Clarice, you are yourself the voices of light, the look, the lightning, the orange flashes surrounding my writing" (*Illa* 1980a, 145). In a non-garden world, "we speak odorless. We live flat, we prosify cold, we eat mute" (*Illa*, 147), for women have been taught "the language that speaks from on high, from afar, which listens to itself, has ears only for itself, the deaf, deafening language that speaks to us from beforehand. They have taught us the language which . . . only listens to its own grammar; and by its order we are separated from things" (*Illa*, 136). This alienating language must be replaced by that of the nourishing female garden. There, Angela gives "lessons of fruit" (*Illa*, 146), of sensual, fertile, generous language: "women need the fruits of women in order to bring the world into the world" (195).

The last section of this last part is entitled, "The re-beginning begins by three . . ." (*Illa* 1980, 198), so that we close the cycle of the mother-the lost daughter-the found daughter, now clearly perceived as inseparable and indeed consubstantial and signified by the recurrent image of the three apples, the three earth apples found in Angela's basket, in a cradle, in loving female hands. They are text-apples, tasting of "the first words harvested from the earth" (*Illa*, 206). They are the fruit of life. Cixous likes the German word *Obst* for fruit, because of its connections with "Obstetrix": midwife, birth-giver. This fruit-Obst ("which signifies both the fruit and the harvest" *Illa*, 194) is not the pomegranate "which they [i.e., the old ones] are always ready to offer us, in order to poison our tongue, and to reduce us, with a seed, to their silence" (127–28),[13] nor is it the poisonous apple of Eden's treacherous tree of knowledge;[14] nor the forbidden fruit of Nietzsche's "gaya scienza," his "Gay Science" preached in the house of male knowledge where women may never cross the threshold (*Newly Born* 1986, 68). Illa's fruit is instead the blessed fruit of "Gay Ignorance" (*Illa*, 211), of brand-new learning-to-come. For Nietzsche, the "gay science" ("die fröhliche Wissenschaft") is "that unity of *singer, knight,* and *free spirit* which distinguishes the wonderful early culture of the Provençals from all equivocal cultures" ([1889] 1969, 333). In other words, it is a rare and splendid harmony between the poet and his society, which enables him to develop fully and to thrive in a harmony which women poets have never yet experienced.

Therefore, since that "knowledge" remains alien to her, and since the female "I" is "not the arena of the known" ("The Character" 1974, 387), woman must be guided by the apple in her hand, and by the hand of the other woman, as by Ariadne's thread, and so step forward "into the ignored, without a *récit* [i.e., a pre-written story], without falling . . . and she writes without foresight, towards what will come, she goes, there are walls and she does not run into them, there are silences and she hears them" (*Illa,* 199).

Illa is then the story, the myth, of "living writing" (1980a, 191), conquered by, for, through, among women. The mythification of women's struggle for access to each other and to seek their own authentic experience is also the mythification of their desire for and eventual access to the Book. Illa enacts the full force of her name, signifying the death (Eurydice)-into-life (Persephone regained) transformation, and is a mythic figure of giving and redeeming. My-themes of Greek, Roman, Egyptian, Judaic, and Christian mythology are recognizable in this mythopoeic amalgam, which also resounds with pell-mell echoes of Virgil, Rilke, Pascal, Valéry, Mallarmé, Nietzsche, Hans Christian Andersen, Derrida, James Joyce, Heine, Heidegger, Blanchot, Kierkegaard, Freud, Racine, and, no doubt, others. Each of these authors is appropriated (sometimes through rejection) and woven into the tapestry of the work. The appropriation and the rejection are part of Illa's work, as all is absorbed into the female project of renewal and creativity.

Cixous's injunction to women to write themselves (the same injunction which Catherine des Roches had already addressed to her contemporaries) is amplified and shown as a possibility through this myth of entrance into the world of the Book. By inventing the female trinity structure, Cixous opens up the closed dyad of the traditional Demeter-Persephone tale in which woman remains enslaved to the law of recurring separation and absence. As Mary Daly remarks, "Persephone had tasted of the pomegranate; she was *possessed* by her husband, and every year when the cold season arrived she went to join him in the deep shadows. The myth expresses the essential tragedy of women after the patriarchal conquest" (1978, 40). Hélène Cixous, in her subversive, converse, treatment of the "old" myth, proposes the possibility of rejecting the pomegranate seed, of breaking the fatal cycle. When Illa is inserted into the myth, mother and daughter—all women—are forever joined. Emancipated from the subterranean laws of silence, women may articulate their own story, their Book. The last words of *Illa* are those of a woman about to give birth/ writing: "I am ready" (1980a, 212).

It is clear that Hélène Cixous goes farther in her ideological and aesthetic use of myth than any of the authors we have previously considered. For her, myth is really the medium in and through which she develops her ideology, and, as we have seen it, enacts her own unified *persona* of woman-teacher-scholar-writer. The use of myth, for Cixous, is much more than a technique of presentation and justification of woman's desire for the Book. Myth is, rather, both the immediate expression of that desire in all its urgency, and the means toward its fulfillment. The mythopoeic process is, for Cixous, a process of recovery and re-formation, as the "old" myths are spirited away from their dead, oppressive contexts, and rejuvenated by reinterpretation, rereading, rewriting, all performed in newly found female contexts. Thus the recuperation of myth corresponds to woman's most fundamental need: that of authentic self-recuperation, of free self-expression, and of uninhibited contact with the self, that female self which had been oppressed and occulted in the stale stories of our cultural past.

Cixous proposes to her women students and readers the equation that to write = to live, and vice versa, and she mythifies that equation into a completely sufficient project of female self-realization, which includes and validates all productive manifestations of "life": motherhood, pleasure, emancipation, fertile bonds with others, creativity in all its forms. Myth allows her to abolish the distance between metaphor and experience, since myth encompasses both. More than any of the earlier writers, Cixous is aware of all the possibilities of myth, and deploys them all to great advantage.

Unlike Marie de France, Marie de Gournay, and Simone de Beauvoir, who invent, consciously or not, myths that fit their particular circumstances, that allow them to deal with their particular problematics of access to the Book, and that help them to surmount the particular obstacles confronting them, Cixous proposes her mythic construct as a possibility—and even the only possibility—for all women. The vast variety and catholicity of her mythemes, which she is able to weave into a seamless tapestry, create a spaciousness that welcomes all women into Cixous's house of myth.

Yet, in spite of the obvious differences between them, we may also see that Cixous has much in common with her predecessors.

The female wild space of Marie de France is echoed almost literally in Cixous. Where the latter founded her notion of female wildness in her readings and rereadings of Freud and Lacan, the former distilled it from her own personal and artistic experience as a woman writer, in an astonishing demonstration of cultural sensitivity and socioartistic intuition. Marie de Gournay's and Simone de Beauvoir's relentless drive towards the Book are not different from the obstinate pulsations Cixous perceives everywhere women are "sous taire," kept in and condemned to silence. But the truly remarkable, almost uncanny, coincidences are those existing between Madeleine and Catherine des Roches on the one hand, and Hélène Cixous on the other.

The mother and the daughter from Poitiers are themselves a living embodiment of Cixous's all-important Ceres-Proserpina relationship, and they even invent Agnodice, who resembles Cixous's Illa, the Third, that is, a restored and restoring bond between women. That bond, as an absolute condition for creativity, motherhood as the archetypal shape of that bond, and life-giving as its archetypal activity are all central, both for the Dames des Roches and for Cixous. In "Agnodice" and in *Illa*, apples signify life, comfort, healing. In both works, the female body is perceived as the site where female experience is generated and inscribed. In both works, the authors address themselves not merely to their own problems and needs, but to those of all women. In both works, women are urged to write, to write themselves, to gain access to the Book from the center of their own specific integrity. Of course, where the Dames des Roches can see their access to the Book only in terms of their period's humanistic, male notions of authorship, Cixous is able to appropriate or reject the givens of her cultural context, and to arrange them into a much freer undertaking than was possible for the women from Poitiers. Nevertheless, the mythic similarities are significant as they reveal identical and persistent impulses toward female solidarity and toward the Book.

Of course, Cixous's language sets her apart from all the earlier writers, as from most of her contemporaries. Through the alliance she creates between the notions of "mythic" and "poetic," she models for herself a language which, although it follows most of the meaning-producing conventions of "ordinary" language, is yet free to deviate from it when the need for a "different" expression— expressive of difference—arises. While Cixous does not reject rational expression in favor of total irrationality, she takes enough liberties to make it clear that rationalism and logic are not her norms, that she aims for a language which is careless of arbitrary limits, and which obeys the call of poetic rather than of rational communication. She rewrites language as she rewrites myth, with the same subversive results.

Cixous's writing, finally, may be seen as the culmination of a long myth-making past, during which women writers have taken up, each in turn, the task of finding access to the promised Book by creating, inventing, or adapting the necessary empowering myths of strength and creative courage.

Notes

1. For Cixous's writings up to 1984, see Conley's bibliography in *Hélène Cixous: Writing the Feminine*.

2. Cixous writes: "What is inscribed under Jean Genêt's name, is the movement of a text that divides itself, pulls itself to pieces, dismembers itself, regroups, remembers itself, is a proliferating, maternal femininity" (*Newly Born* 1986, 84).

3. Cixous names some of the possible confusions (Conley 1984b, 129) the expression may engender. Sandra Gilbert discusses the objections of some American and French feminists to what they see as "the biological essentialism" of concepts such as "fémininité" or "écriture féminine" (1986, xv).

4. Throughout her work Cixous stresses the fact that "I do not equate *feminine* with woman and *masculine* with man" (Conley 1984b, 154), but the realm of the feminine is clearly more accessible and more appealing to women than to most men.

5. The translation is by Smith Palmer Bovie.

6. The translations from *Illa* are mine.

7. In Clarice Lispector's book of short stories, *Family Ties*, there is in the story "Happy Birthday" a young woman, called Cordelia, who, at the birthday party for her eighty-nine-year-old mother-in-law, is the only person in the crowded room to love and understand the old woman. It is likely that this character too has contributed to Cixous's Cordelia.

8. In the short text on the back of *Illa*, Cixous writes: "I have just placed this star on the ground: it is an apple of a text. I have not written it from myself. I wrote it from them [*elles:* feminine plural]. It radiates from us. May I always remember how writing is not self-evident, grows in the constellation formed by giving women."

9. The case of Freud's young patient, Dora, has been used by feminist writers to object to "the authoritarian mode of interpretation and therapy practiced by Freud" (Evans 1982, 65). Cixous has written a play, *Portrait of Dora*, produced in Paris in 1976.

10. Toward the end of the book Angela says; "Eat. This is my earth" (Cixous *Illa* 1980a, 205), words which repeat Christ's invitation: "Eat. This is my body."

11. On this subject, see also Carol Gilligan (1982).

12. Cixous makes it clear that when she exalts the virtue and power of waiting, she is not speaking of patient resignation, but of the energetic present-enhancing waiting which is that of pregnancy.

13. An allusion to the Homeric Demeter-Persephone hymn, according to which Persephone's underworld husband, before letting her go back to her mother, "made her eat a pomegranate seed, knowing in his heart that if she did so she must return to him" (Hamilton 1940, 52). In Cixous's rewriting of the myth, the deadly seed may be refused.

14. For Cixous, the story of the garden of Eden has always been (mis)read from a masculine point of view, as the story of the temptress Eve and victimized man. "The story" insists Cixous "must be re-read from a feminine side. Eve eats the apple, follows the call, the *appel* of the apple, and—she likes it . . . Eve is in rapture and bliss, but her song of innocence was silenced by the Church Fathers" (Conley 1984a, 7).

Hélène Cixous: Works Cited

"The Character of 'Character'." 1974. Trans. Keith Cohen. *New Literary History* 5: 383–402.

"The Laugh of the Medusa." 1976. Trans. Keith Cohen and Paula Cohen. *Signs* 1: 875–93.

"L'Approche de Clarice Lispector." 1979. *Poétique* 10: 408–19.

Illa. 1980a. Paris: des femmes.

"Poetry is/and (the) Political." 1980b. Trans. *Bread and Roses* 2.1: 16–18.

"Castration or Decapitation?" 1981. Trans. Annette Kuhn. *Signs* 7: 42–59.

"August 12, 1980." 1984. Trans. Betsy Wing. *Boundary* 12.2: 8–27.

The Newly Born Woman. 1986. With Catherine Clément. Trans. Betsy Wing. Theory and History of Literature, 24. Minneapolis: University of Minnesota Press.

Works Cited

Armbruster, Carol. 1983. "Hélène-Clarice: Nouvelle Voix." *Contemporary Literature* 24: 145-57.

Bataille, Georges. 1976. "La Part Maudite." In *Œuvres Complètes*, 7: 19-179. Paris: Gallimard.

Bovie, Smith Palmer, trans. 1956. *Virgil's Georgics.* Chicago: University of Chicago Press.

Cameron, Beatrice. 1977. "Letter to Cixous." *Sub-Stance* 17: 159-65.

Conley, Verena Andermatt. 1984a. "Approaches." *Boundary* 12.2: 2-7.

———. 1984b. *Hélène Cixous: Writing the Feminine.* Lincoln: University of Nebraska Press.

———. 1984c. "Voice I . . ." Interview with Hélène Cixous. *Boundary* 12.2: 51-67.

Cook, Albert A. 1980. *Myth and Language.* Bloomington: Indiana University Press.

Corredor, Eva L. 1982. "The Fantastic and the Problem of Re-presentation in Hélène Cixous's Feminist Fixtion." *Papers in Romance* 4: 173-79.

Daly, Mary. 1978. *Gyn/ecology: The Metaethics of Radical Feminism.* Boston: Beacon Press.

Derrida, Jacques. 1976. *Of Grammatology.* Trans. Gayatri Chakravorty Spivak. Baltimore: Johns Hopkins University Press.

Dictionnaire de la Foi Chrétienne. 1968. Ed. Olivier de La Brosse, Antonin-Marie Henry, Philippe Rouillard. Paris: Editions du Cerf.

Duren, Brian. 1982. "Cixous' Exorbitant Texts." *Sub-Stance* 32: 39-51.

Evans, Martha Noel. 1982. "*Portrait of Dora:* Freud's Case History as Reviewed by Hélène Cixous." *Sub-Stance* 36: 64-71.

Féral, Josette. 1980. "The Powers of Difference." In *The Future of Difference.* Ed. Hester Eisenstein and Alice Jardine, 77-94. Boston: G. K. Hall.

Gibbs, Anna. 1979. "Cixous and Gertrude Stein." *Meanjin* 38: 281-93.

Gilbert, Sandra M. 1986. "Introduction: A Tarantella of History." In *The Newly Born Woman* by Catherine Clément and Hélène Cixous. Trans. Betsy Wing. Theory and History of Literature, 24. Minneapolis: University of Minnesota Press.

Gilligan, Carol. 1982. *In a Different Voice.* Cambridge: Harvard University Press.

Graff, Gerald. 1979. *Literature Against Itself: Literary Ideas in Modern Society.* Chicago: University of Chicago Press.

Hamilton, Edith. 1940. *Mythology.* Boston: Little, Brown.

Jardine, Alice A. 1985. *Gynesis: Configurations of Woman and Modernity.* Ithaca: Cornell University Press.

Jones, Ann Rosalind. 1985. "Writing the Body: Toward an Understanding of *l'Ecriture féminine.*" In *The New Feminist Criticism.* Ed. Elaine Showalter. New York: Pantheon Books.

Kogan, Vivian. 1985. " 'I want Vulva!' Cixous and the Poetics of the Body." *L'Esprit Créateur* 25.2: 73–85.

Kuhn, Annette. 1981. "Introduction to Hélène Cixous's 'Castration or Decapitation' " *Signs* 7: 36–40.

Lacan, Jacques. 1966. *Ecrits.* Paris: Editions du Seuil.

_____. 1973. *Les Quatre Concepts fondamentaux de la psychanalyse.* Paris: Editions du Seuil.

Lindsay, Cecile. 1986. "Body/Language: French Feminist Utopias." *The French Review* 60: 46–55.

Lispector, Clarice. 1972. *Family Ties.* Trans. Giovanni Pontiero. Austin: University of Texas Press.

_____. 1978. *Um Sopro de Vida: (Pulsações).* Rio de Janeiro: Editora Nova Fronteira.

Lorde, Audre. 1980. "Poetry is not a Luxury." *The Future of Difference.* Ed. Hester Eisenstein and Alice Jardine, 73–87. Boston: G. K. Hall.

Makward, Christiane. 1976. "Interview with Hélène Cixous." Trans. Ann Liddle and Beatrice Cameron. *Sub-Stance* 13: 19–37.

_____. 1978. "Structures du silence/du délire: Marguerite Duras, Hélène Cixous." *Poétique* 9: 314–24.

Marks, Elaine, and Isabelle de Courtivron, eds. 1980. *New French Feminisms.* Amherst: University of Massachusetts Press.

Mauss, Marcel. 1950. "Essai sur le don: Forme et raison de l'échange dans les sociétés archaïques." In *Sociologie et Anthropologie,* 145–284. Paris: Presses Universitaires de France.

Micha, René. 1977. "La Tête de Dora sous Cixous." *Critique* 33: 114–21.

Nietzsche, Friedrich. (1887) 1974. *The Gay Science.* Trans. Walter Kaufmann. New York: Random House.

_____. (1889) 1969. *Ecce Homo. Nietzsche Werke,* vol. 6. Ed. Giorgio Colli and Mazzino Montinari. Berlin: Walter de Gruyter.

Richman, Michèle. 1980. "Sex and Signs: the Language of French Feminist Criticism." *Language and Style* 13.4: 62–80.

Rossum-Guyon, Françoise van. 1977. "Entretien avec Hélène Cixous." *Revue des Sciences Humaines* 168: 479–93.

Sprengnether, Madelon. 1985. "Enforcing Oedipus: Freud and Dora." *The (M)other Tongue: Essays in Feminist Psychoanalytic Interpretation.* Ed. Shirley Nelson Garner, Claire Kahane, Madelon Sprengnether. Ithaca: Cornell University Press.

Stanton, Domna C. 1980. "Language and Revolution: The Franco-American Dis-Connection." *The Future of Difference.* Ed. Hester Eisenstein and Alice Jardine, 73–87. Boston: G. K. Hall.

Virgil. 1979. *The Eclogues and Georgics.* Ed. R. D. Williams. New York: St. Martin's Press.

*C*onclusion

The French women writers I have studied in this book have all participated in the mythopoeic enterprise according to their specific needs and in response to the desire shared by all of them: to gain access to literary expression, which is, at the same time expression of the Self; to find their own literary voice; to fulfill what Tillie Olsen calls "their ardent intention to write" (1978, 29). As Olsen points out, that intention is fed by contact with the glory and prestige of the literature they have studied. All the authors I have examined were, first, passionate readers, who have heard the appeal, the emphatic voice, emanating from the Book, and who have heard it with extraordinary acuteness.

In exploring the metaphor of the book-reader relationship as friendship, Wayne C. Booth has a hypothetical reader address the Book in these words: "To dwell with you is to grow toward your quality. You lead me first to a level of activity in all ways higher and more intense and in a curious way more fully generous and reciprocal than I am likely to meet anywhere else in the world. And you mold that activity into patterns of longing and fulfillment that make my ordinary dreams seem petty and absurd. You finally thus show what life can be not just to a coterie, a saved remnant looking down on the fools, slobs, and knaves, but to *anyone* willing to work at earning the title of equal and true friend" (1980, 27). These lines—which Marie de Gournay might have addressed to Montaigne, Simone de Beauvoir to George Eliot—evoke and explain the "true" reader's longing for entrance into the world of the Book, and suggest why certain readers, consumed by a desire for admission, might want to make the transition from reading to writing: that is, to an even more passionate and intense communion, motivated by ambition, yearning, rivalry perhaps, certainly love. But in the endeavor of writing, the Book's "irresistible invitation" (Booth 1980, 27) may not extend itself to talented and desirous women as obviously as it does to gifted and ardent male aspiring writers. The traditional expectations and conventions—the deadly mythologies—of Western society have long discouraged women from writing, and, at least to a certain point, continue to do so today, as Olsen and others have demonstrated. Yet each of the authors in this book has found a way to write, and that way is through the use of myth.

Each of these women invents her own myth, using the mythic material present and available in the culture in which she lives. The Celtic material is fashionable in Marie de France's time; Greek and Latin mythology is food and drink to the humanist authors who are the Dames des Roches' contemporaries; the epic material is embedded in France's past, as the Greek is in the French learned tradition, both familiar to Marie de Gournay; Simone de Beauvoir and Hélène Cixous use mythic and literary material known to every educated French person. Yet we may speak of mythic *invention* for these writers, since they use the material at hand as just that: raw material, as paint is to a painter, clay to a sculptor, yarn to a weaver. They take the patriarchal myths and stories apart, as one would a confining, unbecoming, ill-fitting garment, and reassemble them so that the new myths fit *their* particular specifications and individual forms. Female mythopoeic creativity thus goes beyond a superficial adaptation of existing tales. It consists of an energetic, original, and liberating process of remodeling and remaking.

In spite of the evident similarities I have pointed out between Marie de France and Hélène Cixous, or Cixous and the Dames des Roches, the myths I have examined are far from being uniform. Each woman writer must have her own myth, in accordance with the material at her disposition, and with the constraints and problems she has to confront. There is not, there cannot be, *one* myth of the woman writer, since there has not been a consistent, unbroken, culturally recognized tradition, nor an officially established and sanctified institution of women writers. In searching for entrance into the world of literature, as in so many areas of their lives in which they refuse to follow pre-existent patterns (education, work, sexuality, child-care) women must be ingenious, flexible, and diverse in devising appropriate solutions. Cixous, who has made herself into the poet-theoretician of women's access to writing through myth, offers throughout her work an overwhelming variety of mythic figures, new and old, all of whom may be adopted as muses, as givers-of-writing, as guides out of "booby-trapped silence" (*Newly Born* 1986, 93). It is thus not surprising that the myths I have considered in the preceding chapters are obviously different from each other, yet are tied together by a connecting thread: they are all myths of empowerment, intended to assure penetration and eventual acceptance into the world of the Book.

A complete history of female myth making in the domain of the Book, if it were ever written, would necessarily be a record of greatly varying mythic constructs, tied together across the centuries, as our examples show, not by a logic of evolution and progression, but by the persistent and persistently necessary search for creative empowerment and liberation.

Works Cited

Booth, Wayne C. 1980. " 'The Way I Loved George Eliot': Friendship with Books as a Neglected Critical Metaphor." *The Kenyon Review*, n.s., 2.2: 4–27.

Cixous, Hélène, and Catherine Clément. 1986. *The Newly Born Woman*. Trans. Betsy Wing. Theory and History of Literature, 24. Minneapolis: University of Minnesota Press.

Olsen, Tillie. 1978. *Silences*. New York: Delacorte Press/Seymour Lawrence.

$\mathcal{I}$ndex

Notes: n refers to footnotes. Titles
are in *italics*.

Cook, Albert (cited), 35, 127, 128, 129
Correspondence, 43
Cottrell, Robert (cited), 106
Cranston, Mechtild (cited), 116
Curtius, E. R., 20
Cybele, 141

Daly, Mary (cited), 4, 15, 56, 95n3, 129, 139, 145
De Claris Mulieribus (Boccaccio), 58
de Courtivron, Isabelle (cited), 9, 11n5
Demerson, Guy (cited), 46
Demeter-Persephone myth, 136–37, 139, 141, 145, 149n13. See also Persephone
De Raptu Proserpinae (Claudian), 59, 136
Derrida, Jacques, 8, 131, 132, 145
des Roches, Catherine, 44, 138, 145; chastity, 57, 63; education, 47; envy, 59–63; female bonding, 63–64; letters to men, 57; marriage, 57; men, 60; myth, 45, 59; spindle, 52, 67n6; women's education, 51. Works: "L'Agnodice," 59–60, 65; "Chanson des Amazones," 58; "Epistre à sa Mere," 47, 54; Les Missives de Mes-Dames des Roches de Poitiers mere et fille . . . , 57; Les Oeuvres des Mes-dames des Roches de Poetiers mere et fille, 47, 52; "Pour une Mascarade d'Amazones," 58; Les Secondes Oeuvres de Mes-Dames des Roches de Poictiers, Mere & Fille, 51, 53; "To My Spindle," 52–53
des Roches, Dames, 1, 43–67, 140, 154; compared to Hélène Cixous, 147; correspondence, 43; deaths, 67n9; education, 44, 46, 48, 49; envy, 60–63; female bonding, 6; learning and poetry, 45–46; legal rights, 48; men, 57; mother-daughter relationship, 45, 55–57,

58–59, 63; myth, 6, 58, 73; poetic immortality, 45, 54; salon, 43–44; spindle and spinning, 50, 139; women's education, 48
des Roches, Madeleine: education, 47; justification for writing, 47; marriages, 47–48, 67n11; spindle, 50; women and marriage, 49–50; women's education, 48–49, 51. Works: "Epistre à ma Fille," 48, 50; "Epistre aux Dames," 47; Les Missives de Mes-Dames des Roches de Poitiers mere et fille . . . , 56; Les Oeuvres des Mes-dames des Roches de Poetiers mere et fille, 47–50, 54–56, 59; Les Secondes Oeuvres de Mes-Dames des Roches de Poictiers, Mere & Fille, 56
"Les Deus Amanz" (Marie de France), 27–28
Dezon-Jones, Elyane (cited), 75, 95n1
Dido, 132
Diller, George E. (cited), 44, 48, 57, 66n1, 66n2
Discours des Champs Faez (Taillemont), 81–82
Dobbs, Betty Jo (cited), 83–84, 95n5
Dove, Rita (cited), 4
"The Dream of Love: A Study of Three Autobiographies" (Marks), 117
Dronke, Peter, 11n4, 38n3
Duras, Marguerite, 8

Eboissard, François, 47–48
"Egalité des Hommes et des Femmes" (Gournay), 87, 89, 94
Electra, 132
"Eliduc" (Marie de France), 28
Eliot, George, 105, 153
Envy, 59–63, 65
"Epistre à ma Fille" (des Roches, Madeleine), 48, 50
"Epistre à sa Mere" (des Roches, Catherine), 47, 54
"Epistre aux Dames" (des Roches, Madeleine), 47

poets, 3, 7, 55, 65; sexuality, 2; writers, 5, 7–10, 11n4, 17, 22, 25, 67n6, 78, 87, 88, 131–32, 154; writings attributed to male authors, 38n3. *See also* Feminism

"Women's grievance." *See* "Grief des Dames" (Gournay)

Woolf, Virginia, 94

World War I, 108

Writers, 7, 154; male, 5; medieval, 22, 38n3; women, 5, 7–10, 11n4, 17, 22, 25, 67n6, 78, 87, 88, 131–32, 154

Yeats, William Butler, 116

"Yonec" (Marie de France), 28

Zola, Emile, 116

FRENCH WOMEN WRITERS AND THE BOOK

was composed in 10 on 12 Palatino on a Quadex 5000
by BookMasters;
with display type set in Vivaldi
by Dix Type, Inc.;
printed by sheet-fed offset on 50-pound, acid-free Glatfelter Natural Hi Bulk,
Smyth sewn and bound over 88-point binder's boards in Holliston Roxite C
by Braun-Brumfield, Inc.;
with dust jackets printed in two colors
by Braun-Brumfield, Inc.;
and published by
SYRACUSE UNIVERSITY PRESS
SYRACUSE, NEW YORK 13244-5160